In this sculpture there meet more exactly than in any other the unbroken tradition and the sharp renewal of Europe. It is the very type of what is talked of in my book.

The middle statue on the eastern side of the tomb of Philibert of Savoy, at Brou, near Bourg-en-Bresse, it stands upon a site of pre-historic sanctity, yet upon one which felt most fully the spring of the sixteenth century. The south and the north of our civilization mingled in it more thoroughly even than on the Loire. The Walloon and the Italian and the Swiss passed the chisel to each other; Beughen, Vambelli, Meyt were at work there together; and the French of the plains designed and controlled the whole. The church which surrounds it is Gothic, and the last of the Gothic, but the spirit which makes the stone live is the Renaissance.

Its time is just the climax. It was completed perhaps in 1536. Francis, the prince of the arts, was well re-seated on his throne; Marot had yet ten years to live; Rabelais (of an age with him) somewhat more; Ronsard and Du Bellay were boys entering upon their inherit-ance, Calvin's book was printing, Goujon was in his twentieth year.

And all that time is summed up in this figure, which may be a Magdalen, and which I have therefore called "The Beauty of this World."

AVRIL.

The Beauty
of this
World.

AVRIL

BEING

ESSAYS ON THE POETRY OF THE

FRENCH RENAISSANCE

BY

HILAIRE BELLOC

" . . . *Ceux dont la Fantaisie*
Sera religieuse et devote envers Dieu
Tousjours acheveront quelque grant Poesie,
Et dessus leur renom la Parque n'aura lieu."

Essay Index Reprint Series

BOOKS FOR LIBRARIES PRESS
FREEPORT, NEW YORK

First Published 1904
Reprinted 1969

841.09
B446a

69-9840
STANDARD BOOK NUMBER:
8369-1339-6

LIBRARY OF CONGRESS CATALOG CARD NUMBER:
74-99681

PRINTED IN THE UNITED STATES OF AMERICA

CONTENTS

	PAGE
CHARLES OF ORLEANS	1
VILLON	37
MAROT	75
RONSARD	115
DU BELLAY	149
MALHERBE	195

DEDICATION

TO

F. Y. ECCLES

DEDICATION

My dear Eccles,

You will, I know, permit me to address you these essays which are more the product of your erudition than of my enthusiasm.

With the motives of their appearance you are familiar.

We have wondered together that a society so avid of experience and enlargement as is ours, should ignore the chief expression of its closest neighbour, its highest rival and its coheir in Europe: should ignore, I mean, the literature of the French.

We have laughed together, not without despair, to see the mind of England, for all its majesty and breadth, informed at the most critical moments in the policy of France by such residents of Paris as were at the best fanatical, at the worst (and most ordinary) corrupt.

Seeing around us here a philosophy and method drawn from northern Germany, a true and subtle sympathy with the Italians, and a perpetual, just and accurate comment upon the minor nationalities of Europe, a mass of recorded travel superior by far to that of other countries, we marvelled that France in particular should have remained unknown.

We were willing, in an earlier youth, to read this riddle in somewhat crude solutions. I think we have each of us arrived, and in a final manner, at the sounder conclusion that historical accident is principally to blame. The chance concurrence of this defeat with that dynastic influence, the slip by which the common sense of political simplicity missed footing in England and fell a generation behind, the marvellous industrial activities of this country, protected by a tradition of political discipline which will remain unique in

DEDICATION

History; the contemporaneous settling down of France into the equilibrium of power—an equilibrium not established without five hearty civil wars and perhaps a hundred campaigns—all these so separated the two worlds of thought as to leave France excusable for her blindness towards the destinies and nature of England, and England excusable for her continued emptiness of knowledge upon the energy and genius of France: though these were increasing daily, immensely, at our very side.

We have assisted at some straining of such barriers. A long peace, the sterility of Germany, the interesting activities of the Catholic Church, have perhaps not yet changed, but have at least disturbed the mind of the north, and ours, a northern people's, with it. The unity, the passionate patriotism, the close oligarchic polity, the very silence of the English has arrested the eyes of France. By a law which is universal where bodies are bound in one system, an extreme of separation has wrought its own remedy and the return towards a closer union is begun. I do not refer to such ephemeral and artificial manifestations as a special and somewhat humiliating need may demand; I consider rather that large sweep of tendency which was already apparent fifteen years after the Franco-Prussian War. An approach in taste, manners and expression well defined during our undergraduate years, has now introduced much of our inmost life to the French, to us already a hint of their philosophy.

I think you believe, as I do, that the return has begun.

We shall not live to see that fine unity of the west which lent the latter seventeeth and eighteenth centuries their classical repose. No common rule of verse or prose will satisfy men's permanent desire for harmony: no common rule of manners, of honour, of international ethics, of war. We shall not live to see, though we are young now, a Paris reading some new Locke or Hume, a London moved to attentive delight in some latter trinity of Dramatists, some future Voltaire. . . . The high, protected class, which moved at ease between the Capitals of the World, has disappeared; that which

DEDICATION

should take its place is not yet formed. We are both of that one
Faith which can but regard our Christendom as the front of man-
kind and which, therefore, looks forward, as to a necessary goal, to
the re-establishment of its common comprehension. But the rever-
sion to such stability is slow. We shall not live to see it.

It is none the less our duty (if I may use a word of so unsavoury
a connotation) to advance the accomplishment of this good fatality.

Not indeed that a vulgar cosmopolitan beatitude can inspire an
honest man. To abandon one's patriotism, and to despise a frontier
or a flag, is, we are agreed, the negation of Europe. There are
Frenchmen who forget their battles, and Englishmen to whom a
gold mine, a chance federal theory, a colonial accent, or a map, is
more of an inheritance than the delicate feminine profile of Nelson
or the hitherto unbroken traditions of our political scheme. To
such men arms are either abhorrent, or, what is worse, a very
cowardly (and thank God! unsuccessful) method of acquiring or
defending their very base enjoyments. Let us forget them. It is
only as nationalists, and only in an intense sympathy with the highly
individual national unities of Europe that we may approach the
endeavour of which I have spoken.

With us, I fear, that endeavour must take a literary form, but
such a channel is far from ignoble or valueless. He that knows
some part of the letters of a foreign nation, be it but the graces or
even the vagaries of such letters, knows something of that nation's
mind. To portray for the populace one religion welding the west
together, to spread a common philosophy, or to interpret and arrange
political terms, would certainly prove a more lasting labour: but
you will agree with me that mere sympathy in letters is not to be
despised.

We have observed together that the balance in this matter is
heavily against the English. M. Jusserand is easily the first authority
upon popular life in England at the close of the middle ages.
M. Boutmy has produced an analysis of our political development

xiii

which our Universities have justly recognized. Our friend M. Angellier of the Ecole Normale has written what is acknowledged by the more learned Scotch to be the principal existing monograph upon Robert Burns; Mr. Kipling himself has snatched the attention of M. Chevrillon. You know how many names might be added to this list to prove the close, applied and penetrating manner in which French scholars have latterly presented our English writers to their fellow-citizens.

We have both believed that something of the sort might be attempted in the converse; that a view could be given—a glimpse at least—of that vast organism whose foundations are in Rome, coeval with the spring of Christianity, and whose last growth seems as vigorous and as fecund as though it were exempt from any laws of age.

But, I say, we know how heavy is the balance against us.

The Gallic ritual is unrecognized, even by our over-numerous class of clerical antiquarians. The Carolingian cycle is neglected, save perhaps for a dozen men who have seen the Song of Roland. The Complaints of Rustebœuf, the Fabliaux, all the local legendary poetry, all the chroniclers (save Froissart—for he wrote of us), the tender simplicity of Joinville, the hard steel of Villehardouin, no one has handled.

The fifteenth century, the storm of the Renaissance, are not taught. Why, Rabelais himself might be but an unfamiliar name had not a northern squire of genius rendered to the life three quarters of his work.

The list is interminable. Even the great Drama of the great century is but a text for our schools leaving no sort of trace upon the mind: and as for the French moderns (I have heard it from men of liberal education) they are denied to have written any poetry at all: so exact, so subtle, so readily to be missed, are the proportions of their speech.

*   *   *   *   *   *

DEDICATION

If you ask me why I should myself approach the matter, I can plead some inheritance of French blood, comparable, I believe, to your own; and though I have no sort of claim to that unique and accomplished scholarship which gives you a mastery of the French tongue unmatched in England, and a complete familiarity with its history, application and genius, yet I can put to my credit a year of active, if eccentric, experience in a French barrack room, and a complete segregation during those twelve memorable months wherein I could study the very soul of this sincere, creative, and tenacious people.

Your learning, my singular adventure, have increased in us, it must be confessed, a permanent and reasoned admiration for this people's qualities. Such an attitude of mind is rare enough and often dangerous: it is but a qualification the more for beginning the work. It permits us to follow the main line of the past of the French, to comprehend and not to be troubled by the energy of their present, to catch the advancing omens of their future.

Indeed, if anything of France is to be explained in English and to people reading English, I could not desire a better alliance than yours and mine.

But if you ask me why the Renaissance especially—or why in the Renaissance these six poets alone—should have formed the subject of my first endeavour, I can only tell you that in so vast a province, whereof the most ample leisure could not in a lifetime exhaust a tithe, Chance, that happy Goddess, led me at random to their groves.

Whether it will be possible to continue such interpretation I do not know, but if it be so possible, I know still less what next may be put into my hands: Racine, perhaps, may call me, or those forgotten men who urged the Revolution with phrases of fire.

H. BELLOC.

CHELSEA, *January*, 1904.

CHARLES OF ORLEANS.

CHARLES OF ORLEANS.

I PUT down Charles of Orleans here as the first represent-
ative of that long glory which it is the business of this
little book to recall: but to give him such a place at the
threshold requires some apology.

The origins of a literary epoch differ according as that
epoch is primal or derivative. There are those edifices of
letters which start up, not indeed out of nothing, but out
of things wholly different. Produced by a shock or a
revelation, as two gases lit will, in a sharp explosion, unite
to form a liquid wholly unlike either, so after a great conquest, a battle, the sudden preaching of a creed, these
primal literatures appear in an epic or a dithyrambic code
of awful law. Their first effort is their mightiest. They
come mature. They are allied to that element of the
catastrophic which the modern world (taking its general
philosophy from its social condition) denies, but which is
yet at the limits of all things separate and themselves;
accompanies every birth, and strikes agony into every
transition of death.

Those other much commoner epochs in the history of
letters, which may be called derivative, have this current
and obvious quality, that their beginnings merge into
the soil that bred them, also (very often) their decay will

3

lapse imperceptibly into newer things. They are quite definite, but also definitely parented. We know their special stuff and harmony, but we can point out clearly enough the elements which formed that stuff, the tones which unite in that harmony. We can show with dates and citations the parts meeting and blending; our difficulty is not to determine the influences which have mixed to make the general school, but rather to fix the beginning and the end of its effect upon men.

In the first of these the leader, sometimes the unique example of the school, stands out great, but particular and clear, on a background vague or dark. He is as stupendous, yet as sharp and certain, as a mountain facing the morning, with only sky behind. In the second the originator, if there be one, is vague, tentative, perhaps unknown. More often many minor men together introduce a slow and general transition.

Now the French Renaissance has this peculiar mark, that it holds quite plainly by one side of it to the first by the other to the second of these spirits.

It was primal and catastrophic in that it made something completely new. A new architecture, new cities, a new poetry, almost a new language, a new kind of government —ultimately the modern world.

It was derivative in that the shock, the revelation, which produced it, was the return of something allied to the French blood, something rooted in the French memory. Rome surviving or risen had made that Italy, which was

4

now beginning to trouble the Alps, and would surely creep in by every channel of influence, and at last pervade all Europe. Rome, also, in her full vigour, had once framed and ordered Gaul. The French of the Renaissance were woken suddenly, but as they started they recognized the face and the hand of the awakener.

On this account you will find one mind indeed at the very beginning of the change in letters, but not a dominating mind. There is but one man who is certainly an origin, but he is not a master. You see an unique and single personality, distinct but without force, founding no school— the grave, abiding, kind but covert face of Charles of Orleans. He, linked to the French Renaissance, is like the figure of a gentle friend playing in some garden with a child whose manners are new and pleasing to him, but of whose great destiny he makes no guess. That child was to be Du Bellay, Brantome, Montaigne a hundred-sided, huge Rabelais, Ronsard. Or perhaps this metaphor will put it better. To say that Charles of Orleans's equal and persistent music was like a string harped on distinctly in a chorus of flutes and hautboys, till one by one harps from here and there caught up the similar tang of chords and at last the whole body of sound was harping only.

His life was suited to such difference and such origination. Italy, still living, filled him. An Italian secretary wrote from his mouth the most sumptuous of his manuscripts. He banded on Italy as a goal and his Italian land as a legacy to the French crown—to his own son; till (years

5

after his death) the soldiers roared through Briançon and broke the crusted snow of Mont Genèvre. An Italian mother, the most beautiful of the Viscontis, come out of Italy, rich in her land of Asti and her half million of pure gold, had borne him in her youth to the King of France's brother : a man luxurious, over fine, exact in taste, a lover of magnificence in stories and words, decadent in a dying time, very brave. Through that father the Valois blood, unjustly hated or still more unjustly despised according to the varied ignorance of modern times, ran in him nobly.

Take the Valois strain entire and you will find the pomp or rather the fantasy of their great palace of St. Paul; turrets and steep blue roofs of slate, carved woodwork, heavy curtains, and incense and shining bronze. The Valois were, indeed, the end of the middle ages. Some cruelty, a fury in battle, intelligence and madness alternately, and always a sort of keenness which becomes now revenge, now foresight, now intrigue, now strict and terrible government: at last a wild adventure out beyond the hills: Fornovo, Pavia.

Their story is like the manuscripts, which beyond all other things they loved and collected, and which they were the last to possess or to have made; for while it contains in vivid pictures the noblest and the basest subjects: (Joan of Arc and also her betrayal, their country dominant and almost engulfed, Marigano, and then again Pavia) it always glitters with hard enamelled colours against skies of gold, and is drawn and sharp and clean as a thing can be.

Such is the whole line, but look at this one Valois and you see all the qualities of his race toned by a permanent sadness down to a good and even temper, not hopeful but still delighting in beauty and possessed as no other Valois had been of charity. Less passionate and therefore much less eager and useful than most of his race, yet the taint of madness never showed in him, nor the corresponding evil of cruelty, nor the uncreative luxury of his immediate ancestry. All the Valois were poets in their kind; his life by its every accident caused him to write. At fifteen they wedded him to that lovely child whom Richard II had lifted in his arms at Windsor as he rode out in fatal pomp for Ireland. Three years later, when their marriage was real, she died in childbirth, and it is to her I think that he wrote in his prison the ballad which ends:

> Dieu sur tout souverain seigneur
> Ordonnez par grace et douceur
> De l'ame d'elle tellement
> Qu'elle ne soit pas longuement
> En peine souci et douleur.

Already, in the quarrel that so nearly wrecked the crown, the anti-national factions had killed his father. He was planning vengeance, engraving little mottoes of hate upon his silver, when the wars came on them all. A boy of twenty-four, well-horsed, much more of a soldier than he later seemed, he charged, leading the centre of the three tall troops at Agincourt. In the evening of that disaster they pulled him out from under a great heap of the ten thousand dead and brought him prisoner into England, to Windsor then to Pomfret Castle. Chatterton, Cobworth, at last John Cornwall, of Fanhope, were his guardians. To some one of these—probably the last—he wrote the farewell:

Mon très bon hôte et ma très douce hôtesse.

For his life as a prisoner, though melancholy, was not undignified; he paid no allegiance, he met the men of his own rank, nor was he of a kind to whom poverty, the chief thorn of his misfortune, brought dishonour.

Henry V had left it strictly in his will that Orleans the general and the head of the French nationals should not return. For twenty-five years, therefore—all his manhood —he lived under this sky, rhyming and rhyming: in English a little, in French continually, and during that isolation there swept past him far off in his own land the defence, the renewal, the triumph of his own blood: his town relieved, his cousin crowned at Rheims. His river of Loire, and then the Eure, and then the Seine, and even the field where he had fallen were reconquered. Willoughby had lost Paris to Richemont four years before Charles of Orleans was freed on a ransom of half his mother's fortune. It was not until the November of 1440 that he saw his country-side again.

The verse formed in that long endurance (a style which he preserved to the end in the many poems after his release) may seem at a first reading merely mediæval. There is wholly lacking in it the riot of creation, nor can one see at first the Renaissance coming in with Charles of Orleans.

8

Indeed, it was laid aside as mediæval, and was wholly forgotten for three hundred years. No one had even heard of him for all those centuries till Sallier, that learned priest, pacing, full of his Hebrew and Syriac, the rooms of the royal library which Louis XV had but lately given him to govern, found the manuscript of the poems and wrote an essay on them for the Academy.

The verse is full of allegory; it is repetitive; it might weary one with the savour of that unhappy fifteenth century when the human mind lay under oppression, and only the rich could speak their insignificant words; a foreigner especially might find it all dry bones, but his judgement would be wrong. Charles of Orleans has a note quite new and one that after him never failed, but grew in volume and in majesty until it filled the great chorus of the Pleiade— the Lyrical note of direct personal expression. Perhaps the wars produced it in him; the lilt of the marching songs was still spontaneous:

Gentil Duc de Lorraine, vous avez grand renom,
Et votre renommée passe au delà des monts
Et vous et vos gens d'arme, et tous vos compagnons
Au premier coup qu'ils frappent, abattent les Donjons.
Tirez, tirez bombardes, serpentines, Canons!

Whatever the cause, this spontaneity and freshness run through all the mass of short and similar work which he wrote down.

The spring and sureness, the poise of these light nothings make them a flight of birds.

9

CHARLES OF ORLEANS.

See how direct is this:

> Dieu! qu'il la fait bon regarder!
> La gracieuse, bonne et belle.

or this:

> Le lendemain du premier jour de Mai
> Dedans mon lit ainsi que je dormoye
> Au point du jour advint que je sonjeay.

Everywhere his words make tunes for themselves and everywhere he himself appears in his own verses, simple, charming, slight, but with memories of government and of arms.

This style well formed, half his verse written, he returned to his own place. He was in middle age—a man of fifty. He married soberly enough Mary of Cleves, ugly and young: he married her in order to cement the understanding with Burgundy. She did not love him with his shy florid face, long neck and features and mild eyes. His age for twenty-five years passed easily, he had reached his "castle of No Care." As late as 1462 his son (Louis XII) was born; his two daughters at long intervals before. His famous library moved with him as he went from town to town, and perpetually from himself and round him from his retinue ran the continual stream of verse which only ended with his death. His very doctor he compelled to rhyme.

All the singers of the time visited or remained with him—wild Villon for a moment, and after Villon a crowd of minor men. It was in such a company that he recited the last ironical but tender song wherein he talks of his lost youth and vigour and ends by bidding all present a salute in the name of his old age.

So he sat, half regal, holding a court of song in Blois and Tours, a forerunner in verse of what the new time was to build in stone along the Loire. And it was at Amboise that he died.

THE COMPLAINT.

(The 57th Ballade of those written during his imprisonment.)

THE COMPLAINT.

There is some dispute in the matter, but I will believe, as I have said, that this dead Princess, for whose soul he prays, was certainly the wife of his boyhood, a child whom Richard II had wed just before that Lancastrian usurpation which is the irreparable disaster of English history. She was, I say, a child—a widow in name—when Charles of Orleans, himself in that small royal clique which was isolated and shrivelling, married her as a mere matter of state. It is probable that he grew to love her passionately, and perhaps still more her memory when she had died in child-bed during those first years, even before Agincourt, " en droicte fleur de jeunesse,"—for even here he is able to find an exact and sufficient line.

There is surely to be noted in this delicate ballad, something more native and truthful in its pathos than in the very many complaints he left by way partly of reminiscence, partly of poetic exercise. For, though he is restrained, as was the manner of his rank when they attempted letters, yet you will not read it often without getting in you a share of its melancholy.

THE COMPLAINT.

That melancholy you can soon discover to be as permanent a quality in the verse as it was in the mind of the man who wrote it.

THE COMPLAINT.

Las! Mort qui t'a fait si hardie,
De prendre la noble Princesse
Qui estoit mon confort, ma vie,
Mon bien, mon plaisir, ma richesse!
Puis que tu as prins ma maistresse,
Prens moy aussi son serviteur,
Car j'ayme mieulx prouchainement
Mourir que languir en tourment
En paine, soussi et doleur.

Las! de tous biens estoit garnie
Et en droite fleur de jeunesse!
Je pry à Dieu qu'il te maudie,
Faulse Mort, plaine de rudesse!
Se prise l'eusses en vieillesse,
Ce ne fust pas si grant rigueur;
Mais prise l'as hastivement
Et m'as laissié piteusement
En paine, soussi et doleur.

Las! je suis seul sans compaignie!
Adieu ma Dame, ma liesse!
Or est nostre amour departie,
Non pour tant, je vous fais promesse
Que de prieres, à largesse,
Morte vous serviray de cueur,
Sans oublier aucunement;
Et vous regretteray souvent
En paine, soussi et doleur.

17

THE COMPLAINT.

Dieu, sur tout souverain Seigneur,
Ordonnez, par grace et doulceur,
De l'ame d'elle, tellement
Qu'elle ne soit pas longuement
En paine, soussi et doleur.

THE TWO ROUNDELS OF SPRING.

(The 41st and 43rd of the "Rondeaux.")

THE TWO ROUNDELS OF SPRING.

THESE two Rondeaux, of which we may also presume, though very vaguely, that they were written in England (for they are in the manner of his earlier work), are by far the most famous of the many things he wrote; and justly, for they have all these qualities.

First, they are exact specimens of their style. The Roundel should interweave, repeat itself, and then recover its original strain, and these two exactly give such unified diversity.

Secondly: they were evidently written in a moment of that unknown power when words suggest something fuller than their own meaning, and in which simplicity itself broadens the mind of the reader. So that it is impossible to put one's finger upon this or that and say this adjective, that order of the words has given the touch of vividness.

Thirdly : they have in them still a living spirit of reality ; read them to-day in Winter, and you feel the Spring. It is this quality perhaps which most men have seized in them, and which have deservedly made them immortal.

A further character which has added to their fame, is that, being perfect lyrics, they are also specimens of an old-fashioned manner and metre peculiar to the time. They are the resurrection not only of the Spring, but of a Spring

THE TWO ROUNDELS OF SPRING.

of the fifteenth century. Nor is it too fantastic to say that one sees in them the last miniatures and the very dress of a time that was intensely beautiful, and in which Charles of Orleans alone did not feel death coming.

THE TWO ROUNDELS OF SPRING.

Les fourriers d'Esté sont venus
Pour appareillier son logis,
Et ont fait tendre ses tappis,
De fleurs et verdure tissus.
En estandant tappis velus
De verte herbe par le pais,
Les fourriers d'Esté sont venus
Pour appareillier son logis.
Cueurs d'ennuy pieça morfondus,
Dieu merci, sont sains et jolis;
Alez vous en, prenez pais,
Yver vous ne demourrez plus;
Les fourriers d'Esté sont venus.

Le temps a laissié son manteau
De vent, de froidure et de pluye,
Et s'est vestu de brouderie,
De soleil luyant, cler et beau.
Il n'y a beste, ne oyseau,
Qu'en son jargon ne chant ou crie;
Le temps a laissié son manteau
De vent de froidure et de pluye.
Riviere, fontaine et ruisseau
Portent, en livrée jolie,
Gouttes d'argent d'orfavrerie,
Chascun s'abille de nouveau.
Le temps a laissié son manteau.

HIS LOVE AT MORNING.

(The 6th of the " Songs ".)

HIS LOVE AT MORNING.

In this delightful little song the spontaneity and freshness which saved his work, its vigour and its clarity are best preserved.

It does indeed defy death and leaps four centuries: it is young and perpetual. It thrills with something the failing middle ages had forgotten: it reaches what they never reached, a climax, for one cannot put too vividly the flash of the penultimate line, "I am granted a vision when I think of her."

Yet it was written in later life, and who she was, or whether she lived at all, no one knows.

HIS LOVE AT MORNING.

   Dieu qu'il la fait bon regarder
La gracieuse bonne et belle!
Pour les grans biens qui sont en elle,
Chascun est prest de la louer
   Qui se pourroit d'elle lasser!
Tousjours sa beaulté renouvelle.
Dieu, qu'il la fait bon regarder,
La gracieuse, bonne et belle!
   Par deça, ne delà la mer,
Ne sçay Dame ne Damoiselle
Qui soit en tous biens parfais telle;
C'est un songe que d'y penser.
Dieu, qu'il la fait bon regarder!

THE FAREWELL.

(The 310th Roundel.)

THE FAREWELL.

HERE is the last thing—we may presume—that Charles of Orleans ever wrote: "Salute me all the company, I pray."

In that " company " not only the Court at Amboise, but the men of the early wars, his companions, were round him, and the dead friends of his gentle memory.

He was broken with age; he was already feeling the weight of isolation from the Royal Family; he was begining to suffer the insults of the king. But, beneath all this, his gaiety still ran like a river under ice, and in the ageing of a poet, humour and physical decline combined make a good, human thing.

There is an excellent irony in the refrain: " Salute me, all the company," whose double interpretation must not be missed, though it may seem far-fetched.

Till the last line it means, without any question, "Salute the company in my name," but I think there runs through it also, the hint of " Salute me for my years, all you present who are young," and that this certainly is the note in the last line of all. It must be remembered of the French, that they never expand or explain their ironical things, for in art it is their nature to detest excess.

This last thing of his, then, I say, is the most characteristic of him and of his Valois blood, and of the national spirit in general to which he belonged: for he, and it, and they, loved and love contrast, and the extra-meaning of words.

THE FAREWELL.

Saluez moy toute la compaignie
Où à present estes à chiere lie,
Et leur diĉtes que voulentiers seroye
Avecques eulx, mais estre n'y porroye,
Pour Vieillesse qui m'a en sa baillie.

Au temps passé, Jeunesse si jolie
Me gouvernoit; las! or n'y suis je mye,
Et pour cela pour Dieu, que excusé soye;
Saluez moy toute la compaignie
Où à present estes à chiere lie,
Et leur diĉtes que voulentiers seroye.

Amoureux fus, or ne le suis je mye,
Et en Paris menoye bonne vie;
Adieu Bon temps ravoir ne vous saroye,
Bien sanglé fus d'une estroite courroye.

Que, par Aige, convient que la deslie.
Saluez moy toute la compaignie.

35

VILLON.

VILLON.

I HAVE said that in Charles of Orleans the middle ages are at first more apparent than the advent of the Renaissance. His forms are inherited from an earlier time, his terminology is that of the long allegories which had wearied three generations, his themes recall whatever was theatrical in the empty pageantry of the great war. It is a spirit deeper and more fundamental than the mere framework of his writing which attaches him to the coming time. His clarity is new ; it proceeds from natural things ; it marks that return to reality which is the beginning of all beneficent revolutions. But this spirit in him needs examination and discovery, and the reader is confused between the mediaeval phrases and the something new and troubling in the voice that utters them.

With Villon, the next in order, a similar confusion might arise. All about him as he wrote were the middle ages : their grotesque, their contrast, their disorder. His youth and his activity of blood forbad him any contact with other than immediate influences. He was wholly Northern ; he had not so much as guessed at what Italy might be. The decrepit University had given him, as best she could, the dregs of her palsied philosophy and something of Latin. He grew learned as do those men who grasp quickly the

39

major lines of their study, but who, in details, will only be moved by curiosity or by some special affection. There was nothing patient in him, and nothing applied, and in all this, in the matter of his scholarship as in his acquirement of it, he is of the dying middle ages entirely.

His laughter also was theirs: the kind of laughter that saluted the first Dance of Death which as a boy he had seen in new frescoes round the waste graveyard of the Innocents. His friends and enemies and heroes and buffoons were the youth of the narrow tortuous streets, his visions of height were the turrets of the palaces and the precipitate roofs of the town. Distance had never inspired him, for in that age its effect was forgotten. No one straight street displayed the greatness of the city, no wide and ordered spaces enhanced it. He crossed his native river upon bridges all shut in with houses, and houses hid the banks also. The sweep of the Seine no longer existed for his generation, and largeness of all kinds was hidden under the dust and rubble of decay. The majestic, which in sharp separate lines of his verse he certainly possessed, he discovered within his own mind, for no great arch or cornice, nor no colonnade had lifted him with its splendour.

That he could so discover it, that a solemnity and order should be apparent in the midst of his raillery whenever he desires to produce an effect of the grand, leads me to speak of that major quality of his by which he stands up out of his own time, and is clearly an originator of the great renewal. I mean his vigour.

It is all round about him, and through him, like a storm in a wood. It creates, it perceives. It possesses the man himself, and us also as we read him. By it he launches his influence forward and outward rather than receives it from the past. To it his successors turn, as to an ancestry, when they had long despised and thrown aside everything else that savoured of the Gothic dead. By it he increased in reputation and meaning from his boyhood on for four hundred years, till now he is secure among the first lyric poets of Christendom. It led to no excess of matter, but to an exuberance of attitude and manner, to an inexhaustibility of special words, to a brilliancy of impression unique even among his own people.

He was poor; he was amative; he was unsatisfied. This vigour, therefore, led in his actions to a mere wildness; clothed in this wildness the rare fragments of his life have descended to us. He professed to teach, but he haunted taverns, and loved the roaring of songs. He lived at random from his twentieth year in one den or another along the waterside. Affection brought him now to his mother, now to his old guardian priest, but not for long; he returned to adventure—such as it was. He killed a man, was arrested, condemned, pardoned, exiled; he wandered and again found Paris, and again—it seems—stumbled down his old lane of violence and dishonour.

Associated also with this wildness is a curious imperfection in our knowledge of him. His very name is not his own—or any other man's. His father, if it were his father, took his name from Mont-Corbier—half noble. Villon is but a little village over beyond the upper Yonne, near the division, within a day of the water-parting where the land falls southward to Burgundy and the sun in what they call " The Slope of Gold." From this village a priest, William, had come to Paris in 1423. They gave him a canonry in that little church called "St. Bennets Askew," which stood in the midst of the University, near Sorbonne, where the Rue des Ecoles crosses the Rue St. Jacques to-day. Hither, to his house in the cloister, he brought the boy, a waif whom he had found much at the time when Willoughby capitulated and the French recaptured the city. He had him taught, he designed him for the University, he sheltered him in his vagaries, he gave him asylum. The young man took his name and called him " more than father." His anxious life led on to 1468, long after the poet had disappeared.

For it is in 1461, in his thirtieth year, that Villon last writes down a verse. It is in 1463 that his signature is last discovered. Then not by death or, if by death, then by some death unrecorded, he leaves history abruptly—a most astonishing exit! . . . You may pursue fantastic legends, you will not find the man himself again. Some say a final quarrel got him hanged at last—it is improbable : no record or even tradition of it remains. Rabelais thought him a wanderer in England. Poitou preserves a story of his later passage through her fields, of how still he drank and sang with boon companions, and of how, again, he killed a man . . . Maybe, he only ceased to write; took to teaching soberly in the University, and lived in a decent inheritance to see new splendours growing upon Europe. It may very well be, for it is in such characters to desire in early manhood decency, honour, and repose. But for us the man ends with his last line. His body that was so very real, his personal voice, his jargon—tangible and audible things —spread outward suddenly a vast shadow upon nothingness. It was the end, also, of a world. The first Presses were creaking, Constantinople had fallen, Greek was in Italy, Leonardo lived, the stepping stones of the Azores were held—in that new light he disappears.

  *   *   *   *   *   *

Of his greatness nothing can be said; it is like the greatness of all the chief poets, a thing too individual to seize in words. It is superior and exterior to the man. Genius of that astounding kind has all the qualities of an extraneous thing. A man is not answerable for it. It is nothing to his salvation; it is little even to his general character. It has been known to come and go, to be put off and on like a garment, to be lent by Heaven and taken away, a capricious gift.

But of the manner of that genius it may be noted that, as his vigour prepared the flood of new verse, so in another matter his genius made him an origin. Through him first, the great town—and especially Paris—appeared and became permanent in letters.

Her local spirit and her special quality had shone fitfully

here and there for a thousand years—you may find it in Julian, in Abbo, in Joinville. But now, in the fifteenth century, it had been not only a town but a great town for more than a century—a town, that is, in which men live entirely, almost ignorant of the fields, observing only other men, and forgetting the sky. The keen edge of such a life, its bitterness, the mockery and challenge whereby its evils are borne, its extended knowledge, the intensity of its spirit—all these are reflected in Villon, and first reflected in him. Since his pen first wrote, a shining acerbity like the glint of a sword-edge has never deserted the literature of the capital.

It was not only the metropolitan, it was the Parisian spirit which Villon found and fixed. That spirit which is bright over the whole city, but which is not known in the first village outside; the influence that makes Paris Athenian.

The ironical Parisian soul has depths in it. It is so lucid that its luminous profundity escapes one—so with Villon. Religion hangs there. Humility—fatally divorced from simplicity—pervades it. It laughs at itself. There are ardent passions of sincerity, repressed and reacting upon themselves. The virtues, little practised, are commonly comprehended, always appreciated, for the Faith is there permanent. All this you will find in Villon, but it is too great a matter for so short an essay as this.

THE DEAD LADIES.

THE DEAD LADIES.

IT is difficult or impossible to compare the masterpieces of the world. It is easy and natural to take the measure of a particular writer and to establish a scale of his work.

Villon is certainly in the small first group of the poets. His little work, like that of Catullus, like that of Gray, is up, high, completed and permanent. And within that little work this famous Ballade is by far the greatest thing.

It contains all his qualities : not in the ordinary proportion of his character, but in that better, exact proportion which existed in him when his inspiration was most ardent: for the poem has underlying it somewhere a trace of his irony, it has all his ease and rapidity—excellent in any poet —and it is carried forward by that vigour I have named, a force which drives it well upwards and forward to its foaming in the seventh line of the third verse.

The sound of names was delightful to him, and he loved to use it; he had also that character of right verse, by which the poet loves to put little separate pictures like medallions into the body of his writing : this Villon loved, as I shall show in other examples, and he has it here.

THE DEAD LADIES.

The end of the middle ages also is strongly in this appeal or confession of mortality; their legends, their delicacy, their perpetual contemplation of death.

But of all the Poem's qualities, its run of words is far the finest.

THE DEAD LADIES.

Diĉtes moy où, n'en quel pays
Est Flora la belle Rommaine;
Archipiada, ne Thaïs,
Qui fut sa cousine germaine;
Echo, parlant quand bruyt on maine
Dessus riviere ou sus estan,
Qui beaulté ot trop plus qu'humaine?
Mais où sont les neiges d'antan?

Où est la tres sage Helloïs,
Pour qui fut chastré et puis moyne
Pierre Esbaillart à Saint-Denis?
Pour son amour ot cest essoyne.
Semblablement, où est la royne
Qui commanda que Buridan
Fust geĉté en ung sac en Saine?
Mais où sont les neiges d'antan!

Lo Royne Blanche comme un lis,
Qui chantoit à voix de seraine;
Berte au grant pié Bietris, Allis;
Haremburgis qui tint le Maine,
Et Jehanne, la bonne Lorraine,
Qu' Englois brulerent à Rouan;
Où sont elles, Vierge souvraine?
Mais où sont les neiges d'antan!

49

THE DEAD LADIES.

ENVOI.

Prince, n'enquerez de sepmaine
Où elles sont, ne de cest an,
Que ce reffrain ne vous remaine:
Mais où sont les neiges d'antan!

AN EXCERPT FROM THE GRANT
TESTAMENT.

(*Stanzas* 75-79.)

AN EXCERPT FROM THE GRANT TESTA-MENT.

VILLON's whole surviving work is in the form of two rhymed wills—one short, one long : and in the latter, Ballads and Songs are put in each in their place, as the tenour of the verse suggests them.

Thus the last Ballade, that of the " Dead Ladies," comes after a couple of strong stanzas upon the necessity of death —and so forth.

One might choose any passage, almost, out of the mass to illustrate the character of this " Testament" in which the separate poems are imbedded. I have picked those round about the 800th line, the verses in which he is perhaps least brilliant and most tender.

AN EXCERPT FROM THE GRANT TESTAMENT.

LXXV.

Premier je donne ma povre ame
A la benoiste Trinité,
Et la commande à Nostre Dame
Chambre de la divinité;
Priant toute la charité
Des dignes neuf Ordres des cieulx,
Que par eulx soit ce don porté
Devant le trosne precieux.

LXXVI.

Item, mon corps je donne et laisse
A notre grant mere la terre;
Les vers n'y trouveront grant gresse :
Trop luy a fait faim dure guerre.
Or luy soit delivré grant erre :
De terre vint, en terre tourne.
Toute chose, se par trop n'erre,
Voulentiers en son lieu retourne;

LXXVII.

Item, et a mon plus que pere
Maistre Guillaume de Villon
Qui m'esté a plus doulx que mere,
Enfant eslevé de maillon,

AN EXCERPT FROM THE GRANT TESTAMENT.

Degeté m'a de maint boullon
Et de cestuy pas ne s'esioye
Et luy requiers à genoullon
Qu'il n'en laisse toute la joye.

LXXVIII.

Je luy donne ma Librairie
Et le Romman du Pet au Deable
Lequel Maistre Guy Tabarie
Grossa qui est homs veritable.
Por cayers est soubz une table,
Combien qu'il soit rudement fait
La matiere est si très notable,
Qu'elle amende tout le mesfait.

LXXIX.

Item donne à ma povre mere
Pour saluer nostre Maistresse,
Qui pour moy ot doleur amere
Dieu le scet, et mainte tristesse;
Autre Chastel n'ay ni fortresse
Où me retraye corps et ame
Quand sur moy court malle destresse
Ne ma mere, la povre femme!

THE BALLADE OF OUR LADY.

(Written by Villon for his mother.)

THE BALLADE OF OUR LADY.

THE abrupt ending of the last extract, the 79th stanza of the "Grant Testament"—"I give . . ." and then no objective (apparently) added—is an excellent example of the manner in which the whole is conceived and of the way in which the separate poems are pieced into the general work.

What "he gives . . ." to his mother is this "Ballade of our Lady," written, presumably, long before the "will" and put in here and thus after being carefully led up to.

These thirty-seven lines are more famous in their own country than abroad. They pour from the well of a religion which has not failed in the place where Villon wrote, and they present that religion in a manner peculiar and national.

Apart from its piety and its exquisite tenderness, two qualities of Villon are to be specially found in this poem : his vivid phrase, such as :

"*Emperiere des infernaux paluz,*"

(a discovery of which he was so proud that he repeated it elsewhere) or :

"*sa tres chiere jeunesse.*"

And secondly the curiously processional effect of the metre

THE BALLADE OF OUR LADY.

and of the construction of the stanzas—the extra line and
the extra foot lend themselves to a chaunt in their balanced
slow rhythm, as any one can find for himself by reading
the lines to some church sing-song as he goes.

THE BALLADE OF OUR LADY.

Dame des cieulx, regente terrienne,
Emperiere des infernaux paluz,
Recevez moy, vostre humble chrestienne,
Que comprinse soye entre vos esleuz,
Ce non obstant qu'oncques rien ne valuz.
Les biens de vous, ma dame et ma maistresse,
Sont trop plus grans que ne suis pecheresse,
Sans lesquelz biens ame ne peut merir
N'avoir les cieulx, je n'en suis jungleresse.
En ceste foi je veuil vivre et mourir.

A vostre fils diĉte que je suis sienne;
De luy soyent mes pechiez aboluz :
Pardonne moy, comme à l'Egipcienne,
Ou comme il feist au clerc Théophilus,
Lequel par vous fut quitte et absoluz,
Combien qu'il eust au Deable fait promesse.
Preservez moy, que ne face jamais ce
Vierge portant, sans rompure encourir
Le sacrement qu'on celebre à la messe.
En ceste foy je veuil vivre et mourir.

Femme je suis povrette et ancienne
Qui riens ne scay; oncques lettre ne leuz;
Au moustier voy dont suis paroissienne
Paradis faint, où sont harpes et luz,
Et ung enfer où dampnez sont boulluz :

61

THE BALLADE OF OUR LADY.

L'ung me fait paour, l' autre joye et liesse.
La joye avoir me fay, haulte Deesse,
A qui pecheurs doivent tous recourir,
Comblez de Foy, sans fainte ne paresse.
En ceste foy je veuil vivre et mourir.

ENVOI

Vous portastes, digne vierge, princesse,
Jesus regnant, qui n'a ne fin ne cesse.
Le Tout Puissant, prenant notre foiblesse,
Laissa les cieulx et nous vint secourir,
Offrit à mort sa tres chiere jeunesse.
Nostre Seigneur tel est, tel le confesse,
    En ceste foy je veuil vivre et mourir.

THE DEAD LORDS.

THE DEAD LORDS.

As I have not wished to mix up smaller things with greater I have put this *ballade* separate from that of " the Ladies," though it directly follows it as an after-thought in Villon's own book. For the former is one of the masterpieces of the world, and this, though very Villon, is not great.

What it has got is the full latter mediaeval love of odd names and reminiscences, and also to the full, the humour of the scholarly tavern, which was the " Mermaid " of that generation: as the startling regret of:

> Helas! et le bon roy d'Espaigne
> Duquel je ne sçay pas le nom. . . .

and the addition, after the false exit of " je me desiste "

> *Encore fais une question*

He laughed well over it, and was perhaps not thirsty when it was written.

THE DEAD LORDS.

Qui plus? Où est le Tiers Calixte
Dernier decedé de ce nom,
Qui quatre ans tint le papaliste?
Alphonce, le roy d'Arragon,
Le Gracieux Duc de Bourbon,
Et Artus, le Duc de Bretaigne,
Et Charles Septiesme, le Bon? . . . .
Mais où est le preux Charlemaigne!

Semblablement le roy Scotiste
Qui demy face ot, ce dit on,
Vermeille comme une amatiste
Depuis le front jusqu'au menton?
Le roy de Chippre, de renom?
Helas! et le bon roy d'Espaigne
Duquel je ne sçay pas le nom? . . .
Mais où est le preux Charlemaigne!

D'en plus parler je me desiste
Le monde n'est qu'abusion.
Il n'est qui contre mort resiste
Le que treuve provision.
Encor fais une question:
Lancelot, le roy de Behaigne,
Où est il? Où est son tayon? . . . .
Mais où est le preux Charlemaigne!

THE DEAD LORDS.

Où est Claguin, le bon Breton?
Où le conte daulphin d' Auvergne
Et le bon feu Duc d' Alençon? . . . .
Mais où est le preux Charlemaigne!

THE DIRGE.

THE DIRGE.

THIS is the best ending for any set of verses one may choose out of Villon. It follows and completes the epitaph which in his will he orders to be written in charcoal—or scratched —above his tomb: the sad, sardonic octave of "the little scholar and poor." It is a kind of added dirge to be read by those who pass and to be hummed or chaunted over him dead. But it is a rondeau.

See how sharp it is with the salt and vinegar of his pressed courageous smile—and how he cannot run away from his religion or from his power over sudden and vivid beauty.

"Sire—et clarté perpetuelle"—which last are the best two words that ever stood in the vulgar for *lux perpetua.*

It is no wonder that as time went on, more and more people learnt these things by heart.

RONDEAU.

Repos eternel, donne à cil,
Sire, et clarté perpetuelle,
Qui vaillant plat ni escuelle
N'eut oncques, n'ung brain de percil.
Il fut rez, chief, barbe et sourcil,
Comme un navet qu'on ret ou pelle.
   Repos eternel donne à cil.
   Rigueur le transmit en exil
Et luy frappa au cul la pelle,
Non obstant qu'il dit " J'en appelle ! "
Qui n'est pas terme trop subtil.
   Repos eternel donne à cil.

MAROT.

CLEMENT MAROT.

IF in Charles of Orleans the first note of the French Renaissance is heard, if in Villon you find first its energy appearing above ground, yet both are forerunners only.

With Marot one is in the full tide of the movement. The discovery of America had preceded his birth by three or perhaps four years. His early manhood was filled with all that ferment, all that enormous branching out of human life, which was connected with the expansion of Spain; he was in the midst of the scarlet and the gold. A man just of age when Luther was first condemned, living his active manhood through the experience of the great battlefields in Italy, wounded (a valet rather than a soldier) at Pavia, the perpetual chorus of Francis I., privileged to witness the first stroke of the pickaxe against the mediaeval Louvre, and to see the first Italian dignity of the great stone houses on the Loire—being all this, the Renaissance was the stuff on which his life was worked.

His blood and descent were typical enough of the work he had to do. His own father was one of the last set rhymers of the dying Middle Ages. All his boyhood was passed among that multitude of little dry " writers-down of verse " with which, in Paris, the Middle Ages died; they were not a swarm, for they were not living; they were a heap of dust. All his early work is touched with the learned, tedious, unbeautiful industry which was all that the elder men round Louis XII. could bring to letters. By a happy accident there were mixed in him, however, two vigorous springs of inspiration, each ready to receive the new forces that were working in Europe, each destined to take the fullest advantage of the new time. These springs were first, learned Normandy, quiet, legal, well-founded, deep in grass, wealthy; and secondly, the arid brilliancy of the South: Quercy and the country round Cahors. His father was a Norman pure bred, who had come down and married into that sharp land where the summer is the note of the whole year, and where the traveller chiefly remembers vineyards, lizards on the walls, short shadows, sleep at noon, and blinding roads of dust. The first years of his childhood were spent in the southern town, so that the south entered into him thoroughly. The language that he never wrote, the Languedoc, was that, perhaps, in which he thought during all his life. It was his mother's.

It has been noticed by all his modern readers, it will be noticed probably with peculiar force by English readers, that the fame of Marot during his lifetime and his historical position as the leader of the Renaissance has in it something exaggerated and false. One cannot help a perpetual doubt as to whether the religious quarrel, the influence of the Court, the strong personal friendships and enmities which surrounded him had not had more to do with his reputation than his faculty, or even his genius, for rhyme.

Whenever he wanted £100 he asked it of the King with the grave promise that he would bestow upon him immortality.

From Ronsard, or from Du Bellay, we, here in the north, could understand that phrase; from Marot it carries a flavour of the grotesque. Ready song, indeed, and a great power over the material one uses in singing last indefinitely; they last as long as the sublime or the terrible in literature, but we forbear to associate with them—perhaps unjustly —the conception of greatness. If indeed anyone were to maintain that Marot was not an excellent and admirable poet he would prove himself ignorant of the language in which Marot wrote, but let the most sympathetic turn to what is best in his verse, let them turn for instance to that charming lyric: "A sa Dame Malade" or to "The Ballad of Old Time," or even to that really large and riotous chorus of the vine, and they will see that it is the kind of thing which is amplified by music, and which sometimes demands the aid of music to appear at all. They will see quite plainly that Marot took pleasure in playing with words and arranged them well, felt keenly and happily, played a full lyre, but they will doubt whether poetry was necessarily for him the most serious business of life.

Why, then, has he taken the place claimed for him, and why is he firmly secure in the place of master of the ceremonies, as it were, to that glorious century whose dawn he enjoyed and helped to beautify?

I will explain it.

It is because he is national. He represents not what is most this, or most that—" highest," " noblest," " truest," "best," and all the rest of it—in his countrymen, but rather what they have most in common.

Did you meet him to-day in the Strand you would know at once that you had to do with a Frenchman, and, probably, with a kind of poet.

He was short, square in the shoulders, tending in middle age to fatness. A dark hair and beard; large brown eyes of the south; a great, rounded, wrinkled forehead like Verlaine's; a happy mouth, a nose very insignificant, completed him. When we meet somewhere, under cypress trees at last, these great poets of a better age, and find Ronsard a very happy man, Du Bellay, a gentleman; then Malherbe, for all that he was a northerner, we may mistake, if we find him, for a Catalonian. Villon, however Parisian, will appear the Bohemian that many cities have produced; Charles of Orleans may seem at first but one of that very high nobility remnants of which are still to be discovered in Europe. But when we see Marot, our first thought will certainly be, as I have said, that we have come across a Frenchman; and the more French for a touch of the commonplace.

See how French was the whole career!

Whatever is new attracts him. The reformation attracts him. It was *chic* to have to do with these new things. He had the French ignorance of what was foreign and alien; the French curiosity to meddle with it because it had come from abroad; the French passion for opposing, for struggling;—and beneath it all the large French indifference to the problem of evil (or whatever you like to call it), the changeless French content in certitude, upon which ease, indeed, as upon a rock, the Church of Gaul has permanently stood and will continuously repose.

He has been a sore puzzle to the men who have never heard of these things. Calvin (that appalling exception who had nothing in him of France except lucidity) could make neither head nor tail of him. Geneva was glad enough to chaunt through the nose his translations of the Psalms, but it was woefully puzzled at his salacity, and the town was very soon too hot to hold him in his exile. And as for the common, partial, and ignorant histories of France, written in our tongue, they generally make him a kind of backslider, who might have been a Huguenot (and—who knows?—have thrown the Sacrament to beasts with the best of them) save that, unhappily, he did not persevere. Whatever they say of him (and some have hardly heard of him) one thing is quite certain: that they do not understand him, and that if they did they would like him still less than they do.

He was national in the rapidity of the gesture of his mind as in that of his body: in his being attracted here and there, watching this and that suddenly, like a bird.

He was national in his power of sharp recovery from any emotion back into his normal balance.

He was national in that he depended upon companions, and stood for a crowd, and deplored all isolation. He was national in that he had nothing strenuous about him, and that he was amiable, and if he had heard of "earnest" men, he would have laughed at them a little, as people who did not see the whole of life.

He was especially national (and it is here that the poet returns) in that most national of all things—a complete sympathy with the atmosphere of the native tongue. Thus men debate a good deal upon the poetic value of Words-worth, but it is certain, when one sees how bathed he is in the sense of English words, their harmony and balance, that the man is entirely English, that no other nation could have produced him, and that he will be most difficult for foreigners to understand. You will not translate into French or any other language the simplicity of

"Glimpses that should make me less forlorn."

Nor can you translate, so as to give its own kind of grandeur

"Et arrivoit pour bénistre la vigne."

Apart from his place in letters, see how national he is in what he does!

He buys two bits of land, he talks of them continually, sees to them, visits them. They are quite little bits of land. He calls one Clément, and the other Marot! Here is a whimsicality you would not find, I think, among another people.

He has the hatred of "sprawling" in his particular art which is the chief aesthetic character of the French; but he has the tendency to excess in opinion or in general expression which is their chief political fault.

It is thus, then, that I think he should be regarded and that I would desire to present him. It is thus, I am sure, that he should be read if one is to know why he has taken so great a place in the reverence and the history of the French people.

And it is in this aspect that he may worthily introduce much greater things, the Pléiade and Ronsard.

OF COURTING LONG AGO.

(The Eighth of the Roundels.)

OF COURTING LONG AGO.

THIS is a fair enough specimen of Marot at his daily gait: an easy versifier " on a theme " and no more. I have said that it is unjust to judge him on that level, and I have said why; but I give this to give the man as he moved domestically to the admiration of the court and of his friends in a time which missed, for example, the epic character of the last six lines of "Le Beau Tettin," and which hardly comprehended of what value his pure lyric enthusiasms would be to a sadder and drier posterity.

OF COURTING LONG AGO.

Au bon vieulx temps un train d'amour regnoit,
Qui sans grand art et dons se démenoit,
Si qu'un boucquet donné d'amour profonde
S'estoit donné toute la terre ronde:
Car seulement au cueur on se prenoit.

Et si, par cas, à jouyr on venoit,
Sçavez-vous bien comme on s'entretenoit?
Vingt ans, trente ans; cela duroit ung monde
Au bon vieulx temps.

Or est perdu ce qu'amour ordonnoit,
Rien que pleurs fainêtz, rien que changes on n'oyt.
Qui vouldra donc qu'à aymer je me fonde,
Il fault, premier, que l'amour on refonde
Et qu'on la meine ainsi qu'on la menoit
Au bon vieulx temps.

NOËL.

(The Second of the Chansons.)

NOËL.

BUT here, upon the contrary, is the spontaneity of his happy mind; it suggests a song; one can hardly read it without a tune in one's head, so simple is it and so purely lyrical: there is a touch of the dance in it, too.

In these little things of Marot, which are neither learned (and he boasted of learning) nor set and dry (and his friends especially praised his precision), a great poet certainly appears—in short revelations, but still appears. Unfortunately there are not enough of them.

That he thought " like a Southerner," as I have maintained and as I shall show by a further example, is made the more probable from the value he lends to the feminine e. The excellent rhythm of this poem you will only get by giving the feminine e the value of a drawn out syllable:

> " L'effect
> Est faict:
> La bel-le
> Pucel-le," etc.

So Spaniards, Gascons, Provençaux, Italians, rhyme, and all those of the south who have retained their glorious " a's " and " or's."

As for the spirit of it—God bless him!—it is a subject for perpetual merriment to think of such a man's being taken for a true Huguenot and enmeshed, even for a while, in the nasty cobweb of Geneva. But in the last thing I shall quote, when he is Bacchic for the vine, you will see it still more.

NOËL.

Une pastourelle gentille
Et ung bergier en ung verger
L'autrhyer en jouant à la bille
S'entredisoient, pour abréger :
  Roger
  Bergier
  Legière
  Bergière,
C'est trop à la bille joué;
Chantons Noé, Noé, Noé.

Te souvient-il plus du prophète
Qui nous dit cas de si hault faiƈt,
Que d'une pucelle parfaiƈte
Naistroit ung enfant tout parfaiƈt?
  L'effeƈt
  Est faiƈt :
  La belle
  Pucelle
A eu ung filz du ciel voué :
Chantons Noé, Noé, Noé.

95

TWO EPIGRAMS.

(The 41st of the First Book and the 46th of the Second.)

TWO EPIGRAMS.

THESE two epigrams are again but examples of the readiness, the wit, the hard surface of Marot, and they needed no more poetry than was in Voltaire or Swift, but they needed style. It was this absolute and standard style which his contemporaries chiefly remarked in him: the marvel was, that being mainly such an epigrammatist and scholar, and praised and supported only in that guise, he should have carried in him any, or rather so much, fire.

The first was his reply to a Dixaine the king's sister had sent him. The second explains itself.

TWO EPIGRAMS.

Mes créanciers, qui de dixains n'ont cure,
Ont leu le vostre; et sur ce leur ay diſt :
"Sire Michel, sire Bonaventure,
La sœur du Roy a pour moy faiſt ce dit."
Lors eulx cuydans que fusse en grand crédiſt,
M'ont appelé monsieur à cry et cor,
Et m'a valu vostre escript aultant qu'or;
Car promis m'ont non seulement d'attendre,
Mais d'en prester, foy de marchant, encor,
Et j'ay promis, foy de Clément, d'en prendre.

———————

Paris, tu m'as faiſt maints alarmes,
Jusque à me poursuivre à la mort :
Je n'ay que blasonné tes armes :
Un ver, quand on le presse, il mord!
Encor la coulpe m'en remord.
Ne scay de toy comment sera;
Mais de nous deux le diable emport
Celuy qui recommencera.

101

TO HIS LADY IN SICKNESS.

(*The* 16*th Epistle.*)

TO HIS LADY IN SICKNESS.

IT is the way this is printed that makes some miss its value.
It is, like all the best he wrote, a song; it needs the vary-
ing time of human expression, the effect of tone, the repose
and the re-lifting of musical notes; illuminated thus it
greatly charmed, and if any one would know the order of
such a tune, why, it should follow the punctuation: a
cessation at the third line; a rise of rapid accents to the
thirteenth, and then a change; the last three lines of the
whole very much fuller and strong.

So I would hear it sung on a winter evening in an old
house in Auvergne, and re-enter the sixteenth century as
I heard.

TO HIS LADY IN SICKNESS.

Ma mignonne,
Je vous donne
Le bon jour.
Le séjour,
C'est prison.
Guérison
Recouvrez,
Puis ouvrez
Vostre porte
Et qu'on sorte
Vistement ;
Car Clément
Le vous mande.
Va, friande
De ta bouche,
Qui se couche
En danger
Pour manger
Confitures ;
Si tu dures
Trop malade,
Couleur fade
Tu prendras
Et perdras
L'embonpoint.
Dieu te doint,
Santé bonne,
Ma mignonne.

THE VINEYARD SONG.

(The 4th of the Chansons.)

THE VINEYARD SONG.

HERE is Marot's best—even though many of his native critics will not admit it so; but to feel it in full one must be exiled from the vines.

It is a tapestry of the Renaissance; the jolly gods of the Renaissance, the old gods grown Catholic moving across a happier stage. Bacchus in long robes and with solemnity blessing the vine, Silenus and the hobbling smith who smithied the Serpe, the Holy Vineyard Knife in heaven, all these by their diction and their flavour recall the Autumn in Herault and the grapes under a pure sky, pale at the horizon, and labourers and their carts in the vineyard, and these set in the frame of that great time when Saturn did return.

All the poem is wine. It catches its rhymes and weaves them in and in, and moves rapid and careless in a fugue, like the march from Asia when the Panthers went before and drew the car. The internal rhythm and pulse is the clapping of hands in barns at evening and the peasants' feet dancing freely on the beaten earth. It is a very good song; it remembers the treading of the grapes and is refreshed by the mists that rise at evening when the labour is done.

THE VINEYARD SONG.

Changeons propos, c'est trop chanté d'amours,
Ce sont clamours, chantons de la Serpette,
Tous vignerons ont à elle recours,
C'est leur secours pour tailler la vignette.
O serpilette, ô la serpilonnette,
La vignolette est par toy mise sus,
Dont les bons vins, tous les ans, sont yssus!

Le dieu Vulcain, forgeron des haults dieux,
Forgea aux cieulx la serpe bien taillante,
De fin acier, trempé en bon vin vieulx,
Pour tailler mieulx et estre plus vaillante.
Bacchus le vante et dit qu'elle est séante
Et convenante à Noé le bonshom
Pour en tailler la vigne en la saison.

Bacchus alors chappeau de treille avoit,
Et arrivoit pour bénistre la vigne;
Avec flascons Silénus le suivoit,
Lequel beuvoit aussi droiĉt qu'une ligne;
Puis il trépigne, et se faiĉt une bigne;
Comme une guigne estoit rouge son nez.
Beaucoup de gens de sa race sont nez.

RONSARD.

RONSARD.

IF it be true that words create for themselves a special atmosphere, and that their mere sound calls up vague outer things beyond their strict meaning, so it is true that the names of the great poets by their mere sound, by something more than the recollection of their work, produce an atmosphere corresponding to the quality of each; and the name of Ronsard throws about itself like an aureole the characters of fecundity, of leadership, and of fame.

A group of men to which allusion will be made in connection with Du Bellay set out with a programme, developed a determined school, and fixed the literary renaissance of France at its highest point. They steeped themselves in antiquity, and they put to the greatest value it has ever received the name of poet; they demanded that the poet should be a kind of king, or seer. Half seriously, half as a product of mere scholarship, the pagan conception of the muse and of inspiration filled them.

More than that; in their earnest, and, as it seemed at first, artificial work, they formed the French language. Some of its most famous and most familiar words proceed from them—for instance, the word *Patrie*. Some few of their exotic Greek and Latin adaptations were dropped; the greater part remained. They have excluded from French—as some think to the impoverishment of that language—most elements of the Gothic—the inversion of the adjective, the frequent suppression of the relative, the irregularity of form, which had survived from the Middle Ages, and which make the older French poetry so much more sympathetic to the Englishman than is the new—all these were destroyed by the group of men of whom I speak. They were called by their contemporaries the Pleiade, for they were seven stars.

Now, of these, Ronsard was easily the master. He had that power which our anaemic age can hardly comprehend, of writing, writing, writing, without fear of exhaustion, without irritability or self-criticism, without danger of comparing the better with the worse. Five great volumes of small print, all good—men of that facility never write the really paltry things—all good, and most of it glorious; some of it on the level which only the great poets reach here and there. It is in reading this man who rhymed unceasingly for forty years, who made of poetry an occupation as well as a glory, and who let it fill the whole of his life, that one feels how much such creative power has to do with the value of verse. There is a kind of good humility about it, the humility of a man who does not look too closely at himself, and the health of a soul at full stride, going forward. You may open Ronsard at any page, and find a beauty; you may open any one of the sonnets at random, and in translating it discover that you are compelled to a fine English, because he is saying, plainly, great things. And of these sonnets, note you, he would write thirty at a stretch, and then twenty, and then a second book, with seventy more. So that as one reads one cannot help understanding that Italian who said a man was no poet unless he could rap out a century of sonnets from time to time; and one is reminded of the general vigour of the age and of the way in which art of all sorts was mingled up together, when one remembers the tags of verses, just such verses as these, which are yet to be seen in our galleries set down doubtfully on the margin of their sketches by the great artists of Italy.

Ronsard, with these qualities of a leader, unconscious, as all true leaders are, of the causes of his leadership, and caring, as all true leaders do, for nothing in leadership save the glory it brings with it, had also, as have all leaders, chiefly the power of drawing in a multitude of friends. The peculiar head of his own group, he very soon became the head of all the movement of his day. He had made letters really great in the minds of his contemporaries, and having so made them, appeared before them as a master of those letters. Certainly, as I shall quote him in a moment when I come to his dying speech, he was " satiated with glory."

Yet this man did not in his personality convey that largeness which was his principal mark. His face was narrow, long and aquiline; his health uneven. It was evidently his soul which made men quickly forget the ill-matched case which bore it; for almost alone of the great poets he was consistently happy, and there poured out from him not only this unceasing torrent of verse, but also advice, sustenance, and a kind of secondary inspiration for others.

In yet another matter he was a leader, and a leader of the utmost weight, not the cause, perhaps, but certainly the principal example of the trend which the mind of the nation was taking as the sixteenth century drew to a close. I mean in the matter of religion, upon whose colour every society depends, which is the note even of a national language, and which seems to be the ultimate influence beyond which no historical analysis can carry a thinking man.

But even those who will not admit the truth of this should watch the theory closely, for with the religious trend of France is certainly bound up, and, as I would maintain, on such an influence is dependent, that ultimate setting of the French classic, that winding up of the Renaissance, with which I shall deal in the essay upon Malherbe.

The stream of Catholicism was running true. The nation was tumbling back after a high and turbulent flood into the channel it had scoured for itself by the unbroken energies of a thousand years. It is no accident that Ronsard, that Du Bellay, were churchmen. It is a type. It is a type of the truth that the cloth admitted poets; of the truth that in the great battle whose results yet trouble Europe, here,

on the soil where the great questions are fought out,
Puritanism was already killed. The epicurean in them both,
glad and ready in Ronsard, sombre and Lucretian in Du
Bellay, jarred indeed in youth against their vows; but that
it should have been tolerated, that it should have led to no
excess or angry revolt, was typical of their moment. It
was typical, finally, of their generation that all this mixture
of the Renaissance with the Church matured at last into its
natural fruit, for in the case of Ronsard we have a noble
expression of perfect Christianity at the end.

In the November of 1585 he felt death upon him; he
had himself borne to his home as soon as the Huguenot
bands had left it, ravaged and devastated as it was. He
found it burnt and looted, but it reminded him of childhood and of the first springs of his great river of verse. A
profound sadness took him. He was but in his sixty-second
year, his mind had not felt any chill of age. He could not
sleep; poppies and soporifics failed him. He went now in
his coach, now on a litter from place to place in that
country side which he had rendered famous, and saw the
Vendomois for the last time; its cornfields all stubble under
a cold and dreary sky. And in each place he waited for a
while.

But death troubled him, and he could not remain. Within a fortnight he ordered that they should carry him southward to the Loire, to that priory of which—by a custom of
privilege, nobility and royal favour—he was the nominal
head, the priory which is "the eye and delight of Touraine"

—the Isle of St. Cosmo. He sickened as he went. The thirty miles or so took him three painful days; twice, all his strength failed him, and he lay half fainting in his carriage; to so much energy and to so much power of creation these episodes were an awful introduction of death.

It was upon the 17th of November that he reached the walls wherein he was Superior; six weeks later, on the second day after Christmas, he died.

Were I to describe that scene to which he called the monks, all men of his own birth and training, were I to dwell upon the appearance and the character of the oldest and the wisest, who was also the most famous there, I should extend this essay beyond its true limit, as I should also do were I to write down, even briefly, the account of his just, resigned, and holy death. It must suffice that I transcribe the chief of his last deeds; I mean, that declaration wherein he made his last profession of faith.

The old monk had said to him: " In what resolution do you die ? "

He answered, somewhat angrily: "In what did you think? In the religion which was my father's and his father's, and his father's and his father's before him—for I am of that kind."

Then he called all the community round him, as though the monastic simplicity had returned (so vital is the Faith, so simple its primal energies), and as though he had been the true prior of some early and fervent house, he told them these things which I will faithfully translate on account of their beauty. They are printed here, I think, for the first time in English, and must stand for the end of this essay:

He said: "That he had sinned like other men, and, perhaps, more than most; that his senses had led him away by their charm, and that he had not repressed or constrained them as he should; but none the less, he had always held that Faith which the men of his line had left him, he had always clasped close the Creed and the unity of the Catholic Church; that, in fine, he had laid a sure foundation, but he had built thereon with wood, with hay, with straw. As for that foundation, he was sure it would stand; as for the light and worthless things he had built upon it he had trust in the mercy of the Saviour that they would be burnt in the fire of His love. And now he begged them all to believe hard, as he had believed; but not to live as he had lived; they must understand that he had never attempted or plotted against the life or goods of another, nor ever against any man's honour, but, after all, there was nothing therein wherewith to glorify one's self before God." When he had wept a little, he continued, saying, "that the world was a ceaseless turmoil and torment, and shipwreck after shipwreck all the while, and a whirlpool of sins, and tears and pain, and that to all these misfortunes there was but one port, and this port was Death. But, as for him, he carried with him into that port no desire and no regret for life. That he had tried every one of its pretended joys, that he had left nothing undone which could give him the least shadow of pleasure or content, but that at the end he had found everywhere the oracle of Wisdom, vanity of vanities."

He ended with this magnificent thing, which is, perhaps, the last his human power conceived, and I will put it down in his own words:—

"Of all those vanities, the loveliest and most praiseworthy is glory—fame. No one of my time has been so filled with it as I; I have lived in it, and loved and triumphed in it through time past, and now I leave it to my country to garner and possess it after I shall die. So do I go away from my own place as satiated with the glory of this world as I am hungry and all longing for that of God."

DIALOGUE WITH THE NINE SISTERS.

DIALOGUE WITH THE NINE SISTERS.

THIS is a little Amaboean thing not very well known but very Horatian and worth setting down here because it is in the manner of so much that he wrote.

Its manner is admirable. Its gentleness, persistency and increase—are like those of his own small river the Loir. Its last stanza from the middle of the first line " *Ceux dont la fantaisie* " to the end, should, I think be famous; but an English reader can hardly forgive such an introduction as " *Voila sagement dit* " to so noble a finale.

DIALOGUE WITH THE NINE SISTERS.

Ronsard. *Pour avoir trop aimé vostre bande inégale,*
Muses, qui defiez (ce dites vous) le temps,
J'ay les yeux tout battus, la face toute pasle,
Le Chef grison et chauve, et je n'ay que trente ans.

Muses. *Au nocher qui sans cesse erre sur la marine*
Le teint noir appartient; le soldat n'est point beau
Sans estre tout poudreux; qui courbe la poitrine
Sur nos livres, est laid s'il n'a pasle la peau.

Ronsard. *Mais quelle recompense aurois-je de tant suivre*
Vos danses nuiêt et jour, un laurier sur le front?
Et cependant les ans aux quels je deusse vivre
En plaisirs et en jeux comme poudre s'en vont.

Muses. *Vous aurez, en vivant, une fameuse gloire,*
Puis, quand vous serez mort, votre nom fleurira
L'age, de siècle en siècle, aura de vous memoire;
Vostre corps seulement au tombeau pourrira.

Ronsard. *O le gentil loyer! Que sert au viel Homère,*
Ores qu'il n'est plus rien, sous la tombe, là-bas,
Et qu'il n'a plus ny chef, ny bras, ny jambe entiere
Si son renom fleurist, ou s'il ne fleurist pas!

DIALOGUE WITH THE NINE SISTERS.

Muses. *Vous estes abusé. Le corps dessous la lame*
Pourry ne sent plus rien, aussy ne luy en chaut.
Mais un tel accident n'arrive point à l'ame,
Qui sans matière vist immortelle là haut.

Ronsard. *Bien! Je vous suyvray donc d'une face plaisante,*
Dussé-je trespasser de l'estude vaincu,
Et ne fust-ce qu'à fin que la race suyvante
Ne me reproche point qu'oysif j'aye vescu.

Muses. *Vela saigement dit, Ceux dont la fantaisie*
Sera religieuse et devote envers Dieu
Toujours acheveront quelque grand poesie,
Et dessus leur renom la Parque n'aura lieu.

THE EPITAPH ON RABELAIS.

THE EPITAPH ON RABELAIS.

SEVEN years after Rabelais died, Ronsard wrote this off-hand. I give it, not for its value, but because it connects these two great names. The man who wrote it had seen that large and honorable mouth worshipping wine: he had reverenced that head of laughter which has corrected all our philosophy. It would be a shame to pass such a name as Ronsard's signed to an epitaph on such a work as that of Rabelais, poetry or no poetry.

Ronsard also from a tower at Meudon used to creep out at night and drink with that fellow-priest, vicar of the Parish, Rabelais: a greater man than he.

By a memory separate from the rest of his verse, Ronsard was moved to write this Rabelaisian thing. For he had seen him " full length upon the grass and singing so."

There is no need of notes, for these great names of Gargantua, Panurge and Friar John are household to every honest man.

THE EPITAPH ON RABELAIS.

Si d'un mort qui pourri repose
Nature engendre quelque chose,
Et si la generation
Se faiɛt de la corruption,
Une vigne prendra naissance
Du bon Rabelais qui boivoit
Tousjours ce pendant qu'il vivoit;

*   *   *   *   *

Demi me se troussoit les bras
Et se couchoit tout plat à bas
Sur la jonchée entre les tasses
Et parmy les escuelles grasses

*   *   *   *   *

Il chantait la grande massue
Et la jument de Gargantue,
Le grand Panurge et le jaïs
Des papimanes ébahis,
Leurs loix, leurs façons et demeures
Et Frere Jean des Antonneures.
Et d'Espisteme les combas.
Mais la Mort qui ne boivoit pas
Tira le beuveur de ce monde
Et ores le fait boire de l'onde
Du large fleuve d'Acheron.

"MIGNONNE ALLONS VOIR SI LA ROSE."

(The 17th Ode of the First Book.)

"MIGNONNE ALLONS VOIR SI LA ROSE."

"IN these eighteen lines," says very modernly a principal critic, " lies Ronsard's fame more surely than in all the remaining mass of his works." He condemns by implication Ronsard's wide waste of power; but the few other poems that I have here had room to print, should make the reader careful of such judgements. It is true that in the great hoard which Ronsard left his people there are separate and particular jewels set in the copper and the gold, but the jewels are very numerous: indeed it was almost impossible to choose so few as I have printed here.

If it be asked why this should have become the most famous, no answer can be given save the "flavour of language." It is the perfection of his tongue. Its rhythm reaches the exact limit of change which a simple metre will tolerate: where it saddens, a lengthy hesitation at the opening of the seventh line introduces a new cadence, a lengthy lingering upon the last syllables of the tenth, eleventh and twelfth closes a grave complaint. So, also by an effect of quantities, the last six lines rise out of melancholy into their proper character of appeal and vivacity: an exhortation.

Certainly those who are so unfamiliar with French poetry

as not to know that its whole power depends upon an extreme subtlety of rhythm, may find here the principal example of the quality they have missed. Something much less weighty than the stress of English lines, a just perceptible difference between nearly equal syllables, marks the excellent from the intolerable in French prosody: and to feel this truth in the eighteen lines that follow it is necessary to read them virtually in the modern manner—for the "s" in " vesprée" or " vostre " were pedantries in the sixteenth century—but one must give the mute " e's " throughout as full a value as they have in singing. Indeed, reading this poem, one sees how it must have been composed to some good and simple air in the man's head.

If the limits of a page permitted it, I would also show how worthy the thing was of fame from its pure and careful choice of verb—" Tandis que vostre age *fleuronne* "—but space prevents me, luckily, for all this is like splitting a diamond.

"*MIGNONNE ALLONS VOIR SI LA ROSE.*"

Mignonne, allons voir si la rose
Qui ce matin avoit desclose
Sa robe de pourpre au soleil
A point perdu ceste vesprée
Les plis de sa robe pourprée
Et son teint au vostre pareil

Las! Voyez comme en peu d'espace
Mignonne, elle a dessus la place,
Las! Las! ses beautez laissé cheoir!
O vrayment marastre nature,
Puis qu'une telle fleur ne dure
Que du matin jusques au soir!

Donc si vous me croyez, Mignonne,
Tandis que vostre age fleuronne
En sa plus verte nouveauté,
Cuillez, Cuillez vostre jeunesse:
Comme à ceste fleur, la veillesse
Fera ternir vostre beauté.

THE "SONNETS FOR HÉLÈNE"

(The 42nd and 43rd Sonnets of the Second Book.)

THE "SONNETS FOR HÉLÈNE."

HÉLÈNE was very real. A young Maid of Honour to Catherine de Medicis; Spanish by blood, Italian by breeding, called in France " de Sugères," she was the gravest and the wisest, and, for those who loved serenity, the most beautiful of that high and brilliant school.

The Sonnets began as a task; a task the Queen had set Ronsard, with Hélène for theme: they ended in the last strong love of Ronsard's life. A sincere lover of many women, he had come to the turn of his age when he saw her, like a memory of his own youth. He has permitted to run through this series, therefore, something of the unique illusion which distance in time or space càn lend to the aspect of beauty. An emotion so tenuous does not appear in any other part of his work: here alone you find the chastity or weakness which made something in his mind come near to the sadder Du Bellay's: his soul is regardant all the while as he writes: visions rise from her such as never rose from Cassandra; as this great picture at the opening of the 58th Sonnet of the Second Book:

> Seule sans compagnie en une grande salle
> Tu logeois l'autre jour pleine de majesté.

These "Sonnets for Hélène" should be common knowledge:

they are (with Du Bellay's) the evident original upon which
the author of Shakespeare's Sonnets modelled his work:
they are the late and careful effort of Ronsard's somewhat
spendthrift genius.

Here are two of them. One, the second, most famous,
the other, the first, hardly known: both are admirable.

It is the perfection of their sound which gives them their
peculiar quality. The very first lines lead off with a completed harmony: it is as thoroughly a winter night as that
in Shakespeare's song, but it is more solemn and, as it were,
more "built of stone. . . ." "La Lune Ocieuse, tourne si
lentement son char tout à l'entour," is like a sleeping
statue of marble.

To this character, the second adds a vivid interest of
emotion which has given it its special fame. Even the
populace have come to hear of this sonnet, and it is sung to
a lovely tune. It has also what often leads to permanent
reputation in verse, a great simplicity of form. The Sextet
is well divided from the Octave, the climax is clearly under-
lined. Ronsard was often (to his hurt) too scholarly to
achieve simplicity: when, under the clear influence of some
sharp passion or gaiety he did achieve it, then he wrote
the lines that will always remain:

> A fin qu'à tout jamais de siècle en siècle vive,
> La Parfaicte amitié que Ronsard la portait.

THE "SONNETS FOR HÉLÈNE."

XLII

Ces longues nuicts d'hyver, où la Lune ocieuse
    Tourne si lentement son char tout à l'entour,
    Où le Coq si tardif nous annonce le jour,
Où la nuict semble un an à l'ame soucieuse :
Je fusse mort d'ennuy sans ta forme douteuse
    Qui vient par une feinte alleger mon amour,
    Et faisant toute nue entre mes bras séjour
Me pipe doucement d'une joye menteuse.
    Vraye tu es farouche, et fiere en cruauté :
    De toy fausse on jouyst en toute privauté.
        Pres ton mort je m'endors, pres de luy je repose :
Rien ne m'est refusé. Le bon sommeil ainsi
Abuse pour le faux mon amoureux souci.
        S'abuser en Amour n'est pas mauvaise chose.

XLIII

Quand vous serez bien vieille, au Soir à la chandelle,
    Assise aupres du feu, devidant et filant,
    Direz chantant mes vers, en vous esmerveillant,
Ronsard me celebroit du temps que j'estois belle.
Lors vous n'aurez servante oyant telle nouvelle
    Desia sous le labeur à demy sommeillant
    Qui au bruit de mon nom ne s'aille resveillant,
Benissant vostre nom de louange immortelle.

147

THE "SONNETS FOR HÉLÈNE"

Je seray sous la terre et fantôme sans os
Par les ombres myrteux je prendray mon repos.
  Vous serez au foyer une veille accroupie,
Regrettant mon amour et vostre fier desdain.
Vivez, si m'en croyez; n'attendez à demain.
  Cueillez des aujourdhuy les roses de la vie.

DU BELLAY

JOACHIM DU BELLAY.

IN Du Bellay the literary Renaissance, French but trans-figured by Italy, middle-north of the plains but looking southward to the Mediterranean, came to one soul and concentrated upon it, as the plastic expression of the same influence concentrated in Goujon. Very central in time, half soldier, half priest, all student; traveller and almost adventurer, a pilgrim throughout of the Idea, everything about him is symbolic of the generation he adorned.

In its vigour, at least, the Renaissance was a glorious youth—he, Du Bellay, died at thirty-five. Its leap and soaring were taken from the firm platform of strong scholarship—he was a scholar beyond the rest. It fixed special forms—he the French sonnet. It felt the lives of all things running through it as a young man feels them in the spring woods—he gathered in the cup of his verse, and retains for us, the nerve of all that life which is still exultant in the forest beyond his river. His breeding, his high name, his leisured poverty, his passionate friendship, his looking for-ward always to a new thing, a creation—all this, was the Renaissance in person.

Moreover, the Renaissance had in France its seat where,

between rolling lands whose woods are the walls of gardens, the broad and shallow inland Loire runs from Orleans, past Blois and Tours and Saumur, and Ancenis, until near Nantes at last it feels the tide: salt and adventures and the barbaric sea. This varied sheltered land of aged vineyards and great wealth has, for the French Renaissance, the one special quality of beginnings and Edens, namely, that it preserves on to a later time the outward evidences of an original perfection. This place, the nest or seed-plot of the new civilisation, still shows its castles—Blois, Amboise, Chambord. Here Leonardo died, Rabelais, Ronsard himself was born. Here the kings of the Change built in their fantastic pride, and founded a France that still endures. It is as truly the soil of the modern thing as are the provinces north of it (the Isle de France, Normandy, Picardy and Champagne), the soil of the earlier mediaeval flower, and of the Gothic which they preserve unique to our own time.

Now, of this district, Du Bellay was more than a native; he was part of it; he pined away from it; he regretted, as no other man of the time regretted, his father's land: Anjou and the fields of home. He may be said, with some exaggeration, to have died in the misfortune of his separation from the security and sober tradition of his own walls. That great early experience of his, which I have already written down—his meeting with Ronsard—had come to him not far from his own hill, south of the great river. His name, unlike Ronsard's, recalled the gentry of that countryside up to and beyond the beginning of its history; alone of the Pleiade he translated the valley of the Loire, its depth, its delicacy, its rich and subtle loneliness.

Again, the Renaissance lived in France an inspired and an exalted life, so that there necessarily ran through it a fore-knowledge of sudden ending. This tragedy repeated itself in the career of Du Bellay.

His name was famous. The three Du Bellays, the councillor, the soldier, the great Cardinal, were in the first rank of the early sixteenth century. Rabelais had loved them. Francis I. had leaned upon and rewarded their service. His father (their first-cousin and Governor of Brest) was a poor noble, who, as is the fashion of nobles, had married a wife to consolidate a fortune. This wife, the mother of Joachim, was heiress to the house of Tourmélière in Liré, just by the Loire on the brow that looks north-ward over the river to the bridge and Ancenis. In this house he was born. On his parents' early death he inherited the place, not to enjoy it, but to wander. An early illness had made him forsake the career of arms for that of the Church; but Orders were hardly so much as a cloak to him; it is difficult to remember, as one reads the few evidences of his life, that he wore the cloth at all: in his verse all trace of it is entirely absent. He lived still in that lineage which the reform had not touched. The passionate defence of the Catholic Faith, the Assault converging on the church throughout Europe, the raising of the Siege, the Triumph which developed, at last, on the political side the League,

and on the literary the final rigidity of Malherbe, the noise
of all these had not reached his circle, kind, or family.

Of that family the Cardinal seems to have regarded him
as the principal survivor. He had determined to make of
the young poet the heir of its glory. It came to nothing.
He accompanied his relative to Rome: but the diplomacy
of the mission ill-suited him. Of the Royal ladies at court
who befriended him, the marriage of one, the death of
another, increased his insecurity. He had inherited, to his
bane, another estate—Gonor—from his elder brother. It
was encumbered, the cause litigious, and he had inherited
with it the tutelage of a sickly child. He never shook off
the burden. A tragic error marked his end. He died,
certainly broken-hearted, just when his powerful cousin,
by a conversion perhaps unknown to the poet himself, had
rejected calumnies, and had determined to resign to him
the great Archbishopric of Bordeaux.

Eustache Du Bellay, yet another cousin, was Bishop of
Paris. He had made Joachim, on his return from Rome,
a Canon of Notre Dame, and in that capacity the poet,
dying in Paris, was buried in the cathedral. The action of
the Chapter in the eighteenth century, when they replaced
the old tombstones by the present pavement, has destroyed
the record of his grave; I believe it to lie in the southern
part of the ambulatory.

In this abrupt descent, following upon so fierce an activity
of thought, he prefigured, I say, the close of the Renaissance
as his genius typified its living spirit; for all the while, as

you read him, you see the cloud about his head, and the profound, though proud and constant, sadness of his eyes.

This, also, was pure Renaissance in him, that the fields in which he wandered, and which he loved to sing—a man of elegies—were dominated by the awful ruins of Rome. These it was that lent him his gravity, and perhaps oppressed him. He sang them also with a comprehension of the superb.

He was second to Ronsard. Though he was the sharp voice of the Pleiade, though it was he who published their famous manifesto, though his scholarship was harder, though his energy could run more fiercely to one point and shine there more brilliantly in one small climax; yet he was second. He himself thought it of himself, and called himself a disciple. All up and down his works you find an astonished admiration directed towards his greater friend—

> . . . Un amy que les Dieux
> Guydent si hault au sentier des plus vieux.

Or again—

> Divin Ronsard qui de l'arc a sept cordes
> Tiras premier au but de la memoire
> Les traicts ailez de la Françoise gloire.

Everywhere it is his friend rather than he that has touched the mark of the gods and called up from the tomb the ghost of Rome which all that company worshipped.

I say he saw himself that he was second. Old Durat saw it clearly in that little college of poets where he taught the unteachable thing: De Baif, Belleau—all the comrades would have taken it for granted. Ronsard led and was chief, because he had the firm largeness, the laughter and the permanence which are the marks of those who determine the fortunes of the French in letters or in arms. Ronsard made. His verses, in their great mass and unfailing level, were but one example of the power that could produce a school, call up a general enthusiasm, and for forty years govern the taste of his country. There was in him something public, in Du Bellay something domestic and attached, as in the relations of a king and of a herald. Or again, the one was like an ordered wood with a rich open plain about it, the other was like a garden. Ronsard was the Beauce; Du Bellay was Anjou. It might be said of the first that he stood a symbol for the wheat and corn-land of the Vendômois, and of the second, that he recalled that subtle wine of the southern Loire to which Chinon gives the most famous label.

Du Bellay was second: nevertheless, when he is well known in this country it will be difficult to convince Englishmen of that truth. There is in his mind a facet which exactly corresponds to a facet of our own, and that is a quality so rare in the French classics that it will necessarily attract English readers to him: for, of all people, we nowadays criticise most in letters by the standard of our immediate emotions, and least by what was once called "reason." He was capable of that which will always be called "poignancy," and what for the moment we call "depth." He was less careful than are the majority of his countrymen to make letters an art, and so to treat his own personality as a thing apart. On the contrary, he allowed that personality to pierce through continually, so that simplicity, directness, a certain individual note as of a human being complaining— a note we know very well in our own literature—is perpetually discovered.

Thus, in a spirit which all Englishmen will understand, a lightness almost sardonic lay above the depths of his grief, and the tenderness which attached to his home played around the things that go with quietude—his books and animals. I shall quote hereafter the epitaphs he wrote for his dog and for his cat, this singer of sublime and ruined things.

Of the dog who—

> . . . allait tousjours suivant
> Quelquefois allait devant.
> Faisant ne sçay quelle feste
> D'un gai branslement de teste."

and of whom he says, in a pretty imitation of Catullus, that he—

> . . . maintenant pourmeine
> Parmy cette ombreuse plaine
> Dont nul ne revient vers nous.

Or of the cat who was—

> . . . par aventure
> Le plus bel œuvre que nature
> Fit onc en matière de chats.

JOACHIM DU BELLAY.

All that delicate side of him we understand very well.

Nor is it to modern Englishmen alone that he will appeal. He powerfully affected, it may be presumed, the English Renaissance which succeeded him. Spenser—thirty years after his death—was moved to the translation of his famous lament for Rome, and no one can read the sonnets to which he gave their final form without catching the same note in the great English cycle of the generation after him—the close of the sixteenth and the opening of the seventeenth centuries.

But his verse read will prove all this and suggest much more.

EXTRACTS FROM THE "ANTIQUITEZ
DE ROME."

THE "ANTIQUITEZ DE ROME."

OF the high series which Rome called forth from Du Bellay during that bitter diplomatic exile of his, I have chosen these three sonnets, because they seem best to express the majesty and gloom which haunted him. It is difficult to choose in a chain of cadences so equal and so exalted, but perhaps the last, "Telle que dans son char la Berecynthienne" is the most marvellous. The vision alone of Rome like the mother of the Gods in her car would have made the sonnet immortal. He adds to the mere picture a noise of words that is like thunder in the hills far off on summer afternoons: the words roll and crest themselves and follow rumbling to the end: he could not have known as he wrote it how great a thing he was writing. It has all the character of verse that increases with time and seems superior to its own author's intention.

THE "ANTIQUITEZ DE ROME."

III.

Nouveau venu qui cherches Rome en Rome,
   Et rien de Rome en Rome n'apperçois,
   Ces vieux palais, ces vieux arcz que tu vois
Et ces vieux Murs, c'est ce que Rome on nomme.
Voy quel orgueil, quelle ruine, et comme
   Celle que mist le monde sous ses loix
   Pour donter tout, se donta quelquefois,
Et devint proye au temps, qui tout consomme.

   Rome de Rome est le seul monument,
   Et Rome Rome a vaincu seulement.
      Le Tybre seul, qui vers la mer s'enfuit,
   Reste de Rome. O mondaine inconstance!
      Ce qui est ferme, est par le temps destruit,
   Et se qui fuit, au temps fait resistance.

IV.

Celle qui de son chef les estoilles passoit,
   Et d'un pied sur Thetis, l'autre dessous l'Aurore
   D'une main sur le Scythe, et l'autre sur le More,
De la terre, et du Ciel, la rondeur compassoit,
Juppiter ayant peur, si plus elle croissoit
   Que l'orgueil des Geans se relevast encore,
   L'accabla sous ces monts, ces sept monts qui font ore
Tumbeaux de la grandeur qui le ciel menassoit.

163

THE "ANTIQUITEZ DE ROME."

Il luy meist sur le chef la croppe Saturnale
Puis dessus l'estomac assist le quirinale
Sur le ventre il planta l'antique Palatin,
Mist sur la dextre main la hauteur Celienne,
Sur la senestre assist l'eschine Exquilienne
Viminal sur un pied: sur l'autre L'Aventin.

*   *   *   *   *

VI.

Telle que dans son Char la Berecynthienne
Couronnée de tours, et joyeuse d'avoir
Enfanté tant de Dieux, telle se faisoit voir
En ses jours plus heureux ceste ville ancienne:
Ceste ville qui fust plus que la Phrygienne
Foisonnante en enfants et de qui le pouvoir
Fust le pouvoir du Monde, et ne se peult revoir
Pareille à sa grandeur, grandeur si non la sienne.

Rome seule pouvoit à Rome ressembler,
Rome seule pouvoit Rome faire trembler:
Aussi n'avoit permis l'ordonnance fatale,
Qu'autre pouvoir humain, tant fust audacieux,
Se vantast d'égaler celle qui fust égale
Sa puissance à la terre, et son courage au cieux.

THE SONNET OF EXILE.

THE SONNET OF EXILE.

THIS sonnet dates from the same period at Rome, or possibly from his return. It has a different note. It is the most personal and passionate of all his writings, in which so much was inspired by personal regret. On this account it has a special literary interest as the most *modern* thing of the Renaissance. It would be far less surprising to find this written by one of the young republicans under the Second Empire (for instance) than to find a couplet of Malherbe's straying into our time.

THE SONNET OF EXILE.

France, Mère des arts, des armes, et des loix,
    Tu m'as nourry long temps du laiĉt de ta mamelle:
    Ores, comme un aigneau qui sa nourisse appelle,
Je remplis de ton nom les antres et les bois,
Si tu m'as pour enfant advoué quelquefois
    Que ne me respons-tu maintenant, ô cruelle?
    France, France, respons à ma triste querelle:
Mais nul, sinon Echo, ne respond à ma voix.

Entre les loups cruels j'erre parmy la plaine
Je sens venir l'hyver, de qui la froide haleine
    D'une tremblante horreur fait herisser ma peau.
Las! tes autres agneaux n'ont faute de pasture,
Ils ne craignent le loup, le vent, ny la froidure;
    Si ne suis-je pourtant le pire du troppeau.

THE SONNET "HEUREUX QUI COMME ULYSSE."

(The 31st of the " Regrets.")

THE SONNET "HEUREUX QUI COMME ULYSSE."

It was of a large gray house, moated, a town beside it, yet not far from woods and standing in rough fields, pure Angevin, Tourmélière, the Manor house of Liré, his home, that Du Bellay wrote this, the most dignified and perhaps the last of his sonnets. The sadness which is the permanent, though sometimes the unrecognized, moderator of his race, which had pierced through in his latter misfortunes, and which had tortured him to the cry that has been printed on the preceding page, here reached a final and a most noble form: something much higher than melancholy, and more majestic than regret. He turned to his estate, the mould of his family, a roof, the inheritance of which had formed his original burden and had at last crushed him; but he turned to it with affection. If one may use so small a word in connection with a great poet, the gentleman in him remembered an ancestral repose.

There is very much in the Sonnet to mark that development of French verse in which Du Bellay played so great a part. The inversion of the sentence, a trick which gives a special character to all the later formal drama is prominent: the convention of contrast, the purely classical allusion, are mixed with a spirit that is still spontaneous and

173

even naïf. But every word is chosen, and it is especially noteworthy to discover so early that restraint in epithet which is the charm but also the danger of what French style has since become. Of this there are two examples here: the eleventh line and the last, which rhymes with it. To contrast slate with marble would be impossible prose save for the exact adjective "*fine*," which puts you at once into Anjou. The last line, in spite of its exquisite murmur, would be grotesque if the "*air marin*" were meant for the sea-shore. Coming as it does after the suggestions of the Octave it gives you suddenly sea-faring: Ulysses, Jason, his own voyages, the long way to Rome, which he knew; and in the "*douceur Angevine*" you have for a final foil to such wanderings, not only in the meaning of the words, but in their very sound, the hearth and the return.

THE SONNET "HEUREUX QUI COMME ULYSSE"

Heureux qui comme Ulysse a fait un beau voyage
Ou comme cestuy là qui conquit la Toison
Et puis est retourné, plein d'usage et raison,
Vivre entre ses parents le reste de son age!
Quand revoirai-je, hélas, de mon petit village
Fumer la cheminée : et en quelle saison
Revoirai-je le clos de ma pauvre maison,
Qui m'est une province, et beaucoup d'avantage?

Plus me plaist le sejour qu'ont basty mes aieux
Que des palais Romains le front audacieux :
Plus que le mabre dur me plaist l'ardoise fine,
Plus mon Loyre gaulois que le Tybre Latin,
Plus mon petit Lyré que le Mont Palatin,
Et plus que l'air marin la doulceur Angevine.

THE WINNOWER'S HYMN TO THE WINDS.

THE WINNOWER'S HYMN TO THE WINDS.

This delicate air of summer, this reminiscence and comfort for men who no longer see the Eure or the Bievre or any of their northern rivers, this very mirror of Du Bellay's own exiled mind—was written for an " exercise." It is a translation—a translation from the Latin of a forgotten Venetian scholar.

When a man finds in reading such a startling truth, it convinces him that letters have a power of their own and are greater of themselves than the things which inspired them : for when, to show his skill in rendering Latin into French verse, Du Bellay had written this down, he created and fixed for everybody who was to read him from then onwards the permanent picture of a field by the side of a small, full river, with a band of trees far off, and, above, the poplar leaves that are never still. It runs to a kind of happy croon, and has for a few moments restored very many who have read it to their own place; and Corot should have painted it.

THE WINNOWER'S HYMN TO THE WINDS.

A vous troppe legere
Qui d'aele passagere
Par le monde volez,
Et d'un sifflant murmure
L'ombrageuse verdure
Doulcement esbranlez,
   J'offre ces violettes,
Ces lis et ces fleurettes
Et ces roses ici,
Ces vermeillettes roses
Tout freschement escloses,
Et ces œilletz aussi.
   De vostre doulce haleine
Eventez ceste plaine
Eventez ce sejour,
   Ce pendant que j'ahanne
   A mon blé que je vanne
   A la chaleur du jour.

THE FUNERAL ODES OF THE DOG
AND THE CAT.

THE FUNERAL ODES OF THE DOG
AND THE CAT.

HERE are extracts from those two delightful and tender
things to which allusion has already been made. The epitaphs upon his little dog and his little cat.

It was a character in this sad man to make little, humble,
grotesque, pleasing images of grief; as it were, little idols
of his goddess; and he fashioned them with an exquisite
humour and affection. What animal of the sixteenth century lives so clearly as these two? None, I think, except
some few in the pictures of the painters of the low countries.

I wish I had space to print both these threnodies in full,
but they are somewhat long, and I must beg my reader to
find them in the printed works of Du Bellay. It is well
worth the pains of looking.

THE DOG.

THE DOG.

Dessous ceste motte verte
De lis et roses couverte
Gist le petit Peloton
De qui le poil foleton
Frisoit d'une toyson blanche
Le doz, le ventre, et la hanche.

*   *   *   *   *

Son exercice ordinaire
Estoit de japper et braire,
Courir en hault et en bas,
Et faire cent mille esbas,
Tous estranges et farouches,
Et n'avoit guerre qu'aux mousches,
Qui luy faisoient maint torment.
Mais Peloton dextrement
Leur rendoit bien la pareille:
Car se couchant sur l'oreille,
Finement il aguignoit
Quand quelqu'une le poingnoit:
Lors d'une habile soupplesse
Happant la mouche traistresse,
La serroit bien fort dedans,
Faisant accorder ses dens

*   *   *   *   *

THE DOG.

Peloton ne caressoit,
Sinon ceulx qu'il cognoissoit,
Et n'eust pas voulu repaistre
D'autre main que de son maistre,
Qu'il alloit tousjours suyvant :
Quelquefois marchoit devant,
Faisant ne scay quelle feste
D'un gay branlement de teste.

    ✻   ✻   ✻   ✻   ✻

Mon Dieu, quel plaisir c'estoit,
Quand Peloton se grattoit,
Faisant tinter sa sonnette
Avec sa teste folette !
Quel plaisir, quand Peloton
Cheminoit sur un baston,
Ou coifé d'un petit linge,
Assis comme un petit singe,
Se tenoit mignardelet,
D'un maintien damoiselet !

    ✻   ✻   ✻   ✻   ✻

Las, mais ce doulx passetemps
Ne nous dura pas long temps :
Car la mort ayant anvie
Sur l'ayse de nostre vie,
Envoya devers Pluton
Nostre petit Peloton,
Qui maintenant se pourmeine
Parmi ceste umbreuse plaine,
Dont nul ne revient vers nous.

THE CAT

THE CAT

Pourquoy je suis tant esperdu
Ce n'est pas pour avoir perdu
Mes anneaux, mon argent, ma bource:
Et pourquoy est ce donc? pource
Que j'ay perdu depuis trois jours
Mon bien, mon plaisir, mes amours:
Et quoy? ô Souvenance greve
A peu que le cueur ne me creve
Quand j'en parle ou quand j'en ecris:
C'est Belaud, mon petit chat gris:
Belaud qui fust, paraventure
Le plus bel œuvre que nature
Feit onc en matiere de chats:
C'etoit Belaud, la mort au rats
Belaud dont la beauté fut telle
Qu'elle est digne d'estre immortelle.

    *   *   *   *

Mon-dieu, quel passetemps c'estoit
Quand ce Belaud vire-voltoit
Follastre autour d'une pelote!
Quel plaisir, quand sa teste sotte
Suyvant sa queue en mille tours,
D'un rouet imitoit le cours!
Ou quand assis sur le derriere
Il s'en faisoit une jartiere,
Et monstrant l'estomac velu
De panne blanche crespelu,

THE CAT

Sembloit, tant sa trogne estoit bonne,
Quelque docteur de la Sorbonne!
Ou quand alors qu'on l'animoit,
A coups de patte il escrimoit,
Et puis appasoit sa cholere
Tout soudain qu'on luy faisoit chere.

    *   *   *   *

   Belaud estoit mon cher mignon,
Belaud estoit mon compagnon
A la chambre, au lict, a la table,
Belaud estoit plus accointable
Que n'est un petit chien friand,
Et de nuict n'alloit point criand
Comme ces gros marcoux terribles,
En longs miaudemens horribles:
Aussi le petit mitouard
N'entra jamais en matouard:
Et en Belaud, quelle disgrace!
De Belaud s'est perdue la race.

   Que pleust a Dieu, petit Belon,
Qui j'eusse l'esprit assez bon,
De pouvoir en quelque beau style
Blasonner ta grace gentile,
D'un vers aussi mignard que toy:
Belaud, je te promets ma foy,
Que tu vivrois, tant que sur terre
Les chats aux rats feront la guerre.

MALHERBE.

MALHERBE.

THE French Renaissance ended in the Classic. The fate of all that exuberance was to find order, and that chaos of generation settled down to the obedience of unchanging laws. This transition, which fixed, perhaps for ever, the nature of the French tongue, is bound up with the name of Malherbe.

When what the French have entitled "the great time," when the generation of Louis XIV. looked back to find an origin for its majestic security in letters, it was in Malherbe that such an origin was discovered; he had tamed the wildness of the Renaissance, he had bent its vigour to an arrangement and a frame; by him first were explicitly declared those rules within which all his successors were content to be narrowed. The devotion to his memory is nowhere more exalted or more typically presented than in the famous cry—*enfin Malherbe vint.* His name carried with it a note of completion and of an end.

When the romantic revival of our own time sought for one mind on which to lay the burden of its anger, one hard master or pedant who could be made responsible for the drying up of the wells, Malherbe again was found. He became the butt of Hugo's splendid ridicule. He was the god of plaster that could not hear or speak or feel, but which fools had worshipped; a god easy to break to pieces. His austerity—for them without fullness—his meagre output, his solemn reiterated code of "perfect taste," moved them to a facile but intense aggression. He it was that had turned to fossil stone the living matter of the sixteenth century: He that had stifled and killed the spirit they attempted to recall.

This man so praised, so blamed, for such a quality, was yet exactly, year for year, the contemporary of Shakespeare, born earlier and dying later. No better example could be discovered of the contrast between the French and English tempers.

The Romantics, I say, believed that they had destroyed Malherbe and left the Classic a ruined, antiquated thing. They were in error. Victor Hugo himself, the leader, who most believed the classic to have become isolated and past, was yet, in spite of himself, constrained by it. Lamartine lived in it. After all the fantastic vagaries of mystics and realists and the rest, it is ruling to-day with increasing power, returning as indeed the permanent religion, the permanent policy, of the nation are also returning after a century of astounding adventures: for the Classic has in it something necessary to the character of the French people.

Consider what the Classic is and why all mighty civilisations have demanded and obtained some such hard, permanent and, as it were, sacred vehicle for the expression of their maturity.

MALHERBE.

Nations that have a long continuous memory of their own past, nations especially whose gods have suffered transformation, but never death, develop the somewhat unelastic wisdom of men in old age. They mistrust the taste of the moment. They know that things quite fresh and violent seem at first greater than they are: that such enthusiasm forms no lasting legacy for posterity. Their very ancient tradition gives them a thirst for whatever shall certainly remain. The rigid Classic satisfies that need.

Again, you will discover that those whose energy is too abundant seek for themselves by an instinct the necessary confines without which such energy is wasted—and wasted the more from its excess. They canalise for their own security a torrent which, undisciplined, would serve but to destroy. Such an instinct is apparent in every department of French life. To their jurisprudence the French have ever attempted to attach a code, to their politics the stone walls of a Constitution, or, at the least, of a fundamental theory. Their theology from Athanasius through St. Germanus to the modern strict defence against all " liberals " has glorified the unchanging. Every outburst of the interior fires in the history of Gaul has been followed by a rapid, plastic action which reduced to human use what might otherwise have crystallised into an amorphous lava. So the wild freedom of the twelfth century was captured to form the Monarchy, the University, the full Gothic of the thirteenth: so the Revolution permitted Napoleon and produced, not the visionary unstable grandeur of the

Gironde, but the schools and laws and roads and set government we see to-day. So the spring storms of the Renaissance settled, I say, into that steady summer of stable form which has now for three hundred years dominated the literature of the country.

Caught on with this aspect of energy producing the Classic is the truth that energy alone can dare to be classical. Where the great currents of the soul run feebly a perpetual acceleration, whether by novelty or by extravagance, will be demanded; where they run full and heavy, then, under the restraint of form, they will but run more proudly and more strong. It is the flickering of life that fears hard rules in verse and may not feel the level classics of our Europe. Their rigidity is not that of marble; they are not dead. A human acquaintance with their sobriety soon fills us as we read. If we lie in the way of the giants who conceived them (let me say Corneille or the great Dryden), re-reading and further knowledge—especially a deeper experience of common life about us—reveal to us the steadfast life of these images; the eyes open, the lips might almost move; the statue descends and lives.

The man who imposed design and authority and unity upon the letters of his country, and who so closed the epoch with which I have been dealing, was singularly suited to his task. Observant, something of a stoic, uninspired; courageous, witty, a soldier; lucid, critical of method only, he corresponded to the movement which, all around him, was ushering in the Bourbons: the hardening of

Goujon's and de l'Orme's luxuriance into the conventions
of the great colonnades and the sombre immensity of the
new palaces; the return of one national faith to a people
weary of so many random quarrels; the mistrust of an ill-
ordered squirearchy; the firm founding of a central government.

He was Norman. Right of that north whence the vigour,
though not the inspiration, of the Renaissance had pro-
ceeded, and into which it returned. Caen gave him birth,
and still remembers him. Normans still edit his works—
and dedicate these books to the town which also bred
Corneille. Norman, learned with that restrained but
vigorous learning of the province, he was also of the
province in his blood, for he came of one of those fixed
families whose heads held great estates all round Falaise,
and whose cadets branched off into chances abroad : one of
the Boughtons, in Kent, is still "Boughton Malherbe." [1]

He was poor. His father, who held one of those magis-
tracies which the smaller nobility bought or inherited, had
not known where to turn in the turmoil of the central
century. In a moment of distress he called himself
Huguenot when that party seemed to triumph, and Malherbe in anger against the apostasy went down south, a boy
of nineteen, and fought as a soldier—but chiefly duels;
for he loved that sport. He lay under a kind of protection

[1] Not from the Conquest. It is near Charing, originally de Braose
land, but an heiress married a Malherbe in the early twelfth century.

from the great Catholic houses, though still poor, till in 1601—he was a man of forty-six—Henri IV. heard of him. In all these years he had worked at the rule of poetry like an artisan, thinking of nothing else, not even of fame. Those who surrounded him took it for granted that he was a master critic—a sort of judge without appeal, but it was a very little provincial circle surrounding a very unimportant house in Provence. Thus, careless it seems of everything except that " form of language " which was with him a passion, like the academic or theological passions, he was astonished on coming to Paris in 1605 to discover how suited such a pre-occupation was to such a time, and how rapidly he became the first name in contemporary letters. Of men who poured out verse the age was satiated; of men who could seize the language at this turn in its fortune, fix it and give it rules, the age had no knowledge till he came : the age fastened upon him, and insisted upon making him a master.

A full twenty years from 1607 he governed the transformation, not of thought, for that he little changed, but of method and of expression. He decided what should be called the typical metres, the alternative of feminine and masculine in verse, the order of emphasis, the proportion of inversion tolerable, the propriety, the modernity, the archaism of words. It is a function to our time meaningless and futile: to such a period as that, indispensable and even noble. He interpreted and published the national sentiment upon this major thing, the architecture of letters.

The power of his mind, tortured and insufficient in actual production, was supreme in putting forth clearly and finally that criticism which ran as an unspoken and obscure current of opinion in the mind of his age. This was his glory, and it was true.

His dryness was extraordinary. In a life of seventy-two years, during which he wrote and erased incessantly, he, the poet, wrote just so much verse as will fill in large type a little pocket volume of 250 pages; to be accurate, forty-three lines a year. Of this scraping and pumicestone in the mind a better example than his verse is to be found in his letters. A number remain. They might seem to be written by two different men! Half a dozen are models of that language he adored—they cost him, to our knowledge, many days—the rest are slipshod notes that any man might write, for he thought they would not survive, and, indeed, the majority of his editors have had the piety to suppress them.

No one will understand Malherbe who only hears of how, like a dusty workman, he cut and polished, and so fixed the new jewel of letters. In our less happy age the academic spirit is necessarily associated with a lethargic stupidity. In his it was not so. His force, by which this work was carried through, lay in a character of penetration. His face expresses it. His very keen and ready eyes, his high lifted brow, his sharp nose, and the few active lines of his cheek and forehead, the poise of his head, the disdain of his firm mouth, all build him back alive for us. His talk, which stammered in its volubility, was incessant and varied; his temper ready; his bodily command of gesture and definition perfect in old age: he was of good metal all those years.

Of his intense Toryism, his vivacity, his love of arms, his tenacity of perception, Racan gives us in his biography an admirable picture. Just before he died his son was killed in a duel—he, at seventy-two, desired passionately to kill the adversary. "Gambling," he said, "my pence of life against the gold of his twenty-five years." He had wit, and he hated well—hating men after death:

> Here richly with ridiculous display
> Killed by excess was Wormwood laid away,
> While all of his acquaintance sneered and slanged,
> I wept: for I had longed to see him hanged.

His zeal for his tongue was real. As he lay upon his death-bed making his confession after so vigorous a life, he heard his nurse say something to herself which sounded ungrammatical and, turning round from the priest, he put her right in a manner most violent and sudden. His confessor, startled, said: "The time is not relevant." "All times are relevant!" he answered, sinking back. "I will defend with my last breath the purity and grandeur of the French tongue."

To such a man the meaning of the solution at which his people had arrived after a century of civil war lay, above all, in their ancient religion. On that converged those deeper and more permanent things in his soul of which even his patriotism and his literary zeal were but the surface. In the expression of that final solution his verse, which was hardly that of a poet, rises high into poetry; under the heat and pressure of his faith, single lines here and there have crystallized into diamonds. By far the most vigorous of so many frigid odes is the battle cry addressed by him in old age to Louis XIII. setting out against La Rochelle. He visited that siege, but had the misfortune to die a bare week before the fall of the city. The most powerful of his sonnets, or rather the only powerful one, is that in which he calls to Our Lord for vengeance against the men who killed his son. Catholicism in its every effect, political and personal, as it were literary too, possessed the man, so that in ending the types of the French Renaissance with him you see how the terms in which ultimately the French express themselves are and will remain religious. The last two lines of his most famous and most Catholic poem have about them just that sound which saves them, in spite of their too simple words, from falling into the vulgar commonplace of vague and creedless men. In writing them down one seems to be writing down the fate of the great century now tamed, alas! and ordered, as must be the violence of over-human things:—

Vouloir ce que Dieu veut est la seule Science
Qui nous met en repos.

EXTRACTS.

(From the " Ode to Louis XIII. setting out against La Rochelle," and the " Sonnet on his son's death.")

EXTRACTS.

IT has been remarked that Malherbe in his most vigorous years deliberately employed the strength of his mind to the repression of emotion in his verse, and used it only to fashion, guide, control, and at last fix permanently the rules of the language. It is certainly true that as his bodily vigour declined, a certain unexpected anger and violence enters into his verse, to the great relief of us moderns: not to that of his contemporaries.

Of this feature in him, the two following extracts are sufficient proof. They were written, the first at the close of his seventy-second, the other at the entry of his seventy-third year. In each, something close to his heart was at issue, and in each he gives some vent—far more than had been his wont—to passion.

The first is a cry to Louis XIII. to have done with the Huguenot. It was written to the camp before La Rochelle. I know of nothing in French literature which more expresses the intense current of national feeling against the nobility and rich townsmen who had attempted to warp the national tradition and who had re-introduced into French life the element which France works perpetually to throw out as un-European, ill-cultured and evil. Indeed, the reading of it is of more value to the comprehension of the national attitude than any set history you may read.

The second is in its way a thing equally religious and equally catholic. This call for vengeance to God was not only an expression of anger called forth by his son's death, it was also, and very largely, the effect of a reaction against the ethics of Geneva: an attack on the idolatry at once of meekness and of fatality which was to him so intolerable a corruption of the Christian religion.

There is some doubt as to whether it is his last work. I believe it to be so; but Blaise, in his excellent edition, prints the dull and unreadable ode to Lagade later, and ascribes it to the same year.

ODE TO LOUIS XIII.

Fais choir en sacrifice au démon de la France
Les fronts trop élevés de ces ames d'enfer;
Et n'épargne contre eux, pour notre délivrance,
*   Ni le feu ni le fer.*

Assez de leurs complots l'infidéle malice
A nourri le désordre et la sédition:
Quitte le nom de Juste, ou fais voir ta justice
*   En leur punition.*

Le centième décembre a les plaines ternies,
Et le centieme avril les a peintes de fleurs,
Depuis que parmi nous leurs brutales manies
*   Ne causent que des pleurs.*

Dans toutes les fureurs des siècles de tes pères,
Les monstres les plus noirs firent-ils jamais rien
Que l'inhumanité de ces cœurs de vipères
*   Ne renouvelle au tien?*

Par qui sont aujourd'hui tant de villes desertes,
Tant de grands bâtiments en masures changes,
Et de tant de chardons les campagnes couvertes,
*   Que par ces enrages?*

✳   ✳   ✳   ✳   ✳

ODE TO LOUIS XIII.

Marche, va les détruire, eteins-en la semence,
Et suis jusqu'à leur fin ton courroux généreux,
Sans jamais ecouter ni pitié ni clémence
*   Qui te parle pour eux.*

*   *   *   *   *

Toutes les autres morts n'ont mérite ni marque;
Celle-ci porte seule un éclat radieux,
Qui fait revivre l'homme, et le met de la barque
*   A la table des dieux.*

SONNET ON HIS SON'S DEATH.

SONNET ON HIS SON'S DEATH.

Que mon fils ait perdu sa depouille mortelle,
Ce fils qui fut si brave, et que j'aimai si fort,
Je ne l'impute point à l'injure du sort,
Puis que finir à l'homme est chose naturelle.

Mais que de deux marauds la surprise infidéle
Ait terminé ses jours d'une tragique mort,
En cela ma douleur n'a point de reconfort,
Et tous mes sentiments sont d'accord avec elle.

O mon Dieu, mon Sauveur, puisque, par la raison,
Le trouble de mon ame étant sans guérison,
Le vœu de la vengeance est un vœu légitime,

Fais que de ton appui je sois fortifié;
Ta justice t'en prie, et les auteurs du crime
Sont fils de ces bourreaux qui t'ont crucifié.

EXTRACTS FROM
THE "CONSOLATION OF DU PERRIER."

THE "CONSOLATION OF DU PERRIER."

THESE stanzas, which are among the best-known as they are, in the opinion of many, the dullest, in French literature, serve well to close this book.

One verse at least (the fourth) is most legitimately famous, though it is hackneyed from the constant repetition of fools. For the rest a certain simplicity, a great precision, may or may not atone for their deliberate coldness.

What is certain is that, poetry or not, they admirably express the spirit of his pen and its prodigious effect. They express the classical end of the French Renaissance with as much weight and hardness as the great blank walls of stone that were beginning to show in the rebuilding of Paris. It is for this quality that I have printed them here, using them as the definite term of that long, glorious, and uncertain phase in European letters.

THE "CONSOLATION OF DU PERRIER."

Ta douleur, du Perrier, sera donc éternelle?
    Et les tristes discours
Que te met en l'esprit l'amitié paternelle
    L'augmenteront toujours?

Le malheur de ta fille au tombeau descendue
    Par un commun trépas,
Est-ce quelque dédale où ta raison perdue
    Ne se retrouve pas?

Je sais de quels appas son enfance étoit pleine,
    Et n'ai pas entrepris,
Injurieux ami, de soulager ta peine
    Avecque son mépris.

Mais elle étoit du monde, où les plus belles choses
    Ont le pire destin;
Et rose elle a vécu ce que vivent les roses
    L'espace d'un matin.

Puis quand ainsi seroit que, selon ta priere,
    Elle auroit obtenu
D'avoir en cheveux blancs terminé sa carrière,
    Qu'en fût-il avenu?

Penses-tu que, plus vieille, en la maison celeste
    Elle eût eu plus d'accueil,
Ou qu'elle eût moins senti la poussière funeste
    Et les vers du cercueil?

       *   *   *   *

THE "CONSOLATION OF DU PERRIER."

De moi, déja deux fois d'une pareille foudre
  Je me suis vu perclus;
Et deux fois la raison m'a si bien fait résoudre,
  Qu'il ne m'en souvient plus.

Non qu'il ne me soit mal que la tombe posséde
  Ce qui me fut si cher;
Mais en un accident qui n'a point de reméde,
  Il n'en faut point chercher.

La Mort a des rigueurs à nulle autre pareilles:
  On a beau la prier;
La cruelle qu'elle est se bouche les oreilles,
  Et nous laisse crier.

Le pauvre en sa cabane, où le chaume le couvre,
  Est sujet à ses lois;
Et la garde qui veille aux barrières du Louvre
  N'en défend point nos rois.

De murmurer contre elle et perdre patience,
  Il est mal à propos;
Vouloir ce que Dieu veut est la seule science
  Qui nous met en repos.

" *Vouloir ce que Dieu veut est la seule science*
Qui nous met en repos."

NOTES.

NOTES.

CHARLES OF ORLEANS.

THE COMPLAINT.

Line 5. *Prins.* An inaccurate pedantic past participle of *prendre.*

Line 14. *Faulse.* There is to be noted here and elsewhere throughout these extracts, until the modern spelling at the close of the period, the redundant "l" in many words. It was an effect of pure pedantry. The latin "l" had become *u* in northern French. *Falsa* made, naturally, "Fausse." The partial learning of the later middle ages reintroduced an "l" which was not known to be transformed, but was thought omitted.

Line 24. *Liesse.* One of the commonest words of this epoch, lost to modern French. It means joy = *laetitia.*

Line 25. Note the gender of "Amour," feminine even in the singular throughout the middle ages and renaissance—right up to the seventeenth century.

THE TWO ROUNDELS OF SPRING.

I

Line 1. *Fourriers.* The servants who go before to find lodging. The term survives in French military terminology. The *Fourriers* are the non-commissioned officers and party who go forward and mark the Billeting of a regiment.

Line 9. *Pieça* = *il y a pièce* ; "lately". *Cf. naguère* = "*il n'y a guère.* . . ."

Line 11. *Prenez pais* = "take the fields," begone.

227

NOTES.

Line 19. Note "*Chant*," the regular form of the subjunctive =
Cantet. The only latin vowel preserved after the tonic syllable is a =
French e (mute). Thus *contat*="chante" which form has in modern
French usurped the subjunctive.

Line 23. *Livrée*="Liberata," *i.e.*, things given out. A term originally applied not only to clothing, but to the general allowance of the
king's household. Hence our word "livery."

The Farewell.

Line 2. *Chiere lie.* "Happy countenance." *Chiere* here is the
substantive, *lie*=*laeta*, is the adjectve. *Bonne chère* means "a good time"
where *chère* is an old word for "head" ($\kappa\alpha\rho\alpha$).

Line 5. *Baillie*=Bailliwick, "For Age that has me now within her
bounds."

Line 7. *Mye.* "Crumb." "I am not a whit (not a crumb) with her
(*Joie*) to-day."

Line 15. "Well braced," literally "well girthed" (as a horse is).

VILLON.

The Dead Ladies.

Stanza 1, line 1. Note the redundant negative; it is characteristic
of mediaeval French, as of all primitive work, that the general sugges-
tion of doubt is sufficient to justify a redundant negative.

Line 2. *Flora*, etc. It is worth while knowing who these women
were. *Flora* is Juvenal's Flora (Sat. II. 9), a legend in the university. Of
Archipiada I know nothing. *Thaïs* was certainly the Egyptian courtesan
turned anchoress and canonized, famous in the middle ages and revived
to-day in the repulsive masterpiece of M. Anatole France. *Elois* is, of
course, *Heloïse*, and *Esbaillart* is Abelard. The queen, who in the
legend had Buridan (and many others) drowned, was the Dowager of
Burgundy that lived in the Tour de Nesle, where the Palais Mazarin

is now, and had half the university for a lover: in sober history she founded that college of Burgundy from which the Ecole de Médecine is descended; the legend about her is first heard of (save in this poem) in 1471, from the pen of a German in Leipzig. *Blanche* may be Blanche of Castille, but more likely she was a vision of Villon's own, for what did St. Louis' mother ever sing? *Berte* is the legendary mother of Charlemagne in the Epics; *Beatris* is any Beatrice you choose, for they have all died. *Allis* may just possibly be one of the Troubadour heroines, more likely she is here introduced for rhyme and metre; *Haremburgis* is strictly historical: she was the Heiress of Maine who married Foulque of Anjou in 1110 and died in 1126: an ancestress, therefore, of the Plantagenets. *Jehanne* is, of course, Joan of Arc.

Line 8. *D'Antan* is *not* "Yester-year." It is "Ante annum," all time past before *this* year. Rossetti's "Yester-year" moreover, is an absurd and affected neologism; "Antan" is an excellent and living French word.

Stanza II., line 2. Note the pronunciation of "Moyne" to rhyme (more or less) with "eine": the oi, ai and ei sounds were very similar till the sixteenth century at earliest. They are interchangeable in many popular provincialisms and in some words, *e.g.*, Fouet, pronounced "Foit" the same tendency survives. The transition began in the beginning of the seventeenth century as we learn from Vaugelas: and the influence towards the modern sound came from the Court.

Stanza III., line 2. *Seraine* = "Syren."

Line 5. "*Jehanne*," "*Jehan*," in spite of the classical survival in their spelling, were monosyllables from the earliest times.

Line 7. The "*elles*" here would not scan but for the elided "e" in "*souv'raine*" at the end of the line. In some editions "*ils*" is found and *souveraine* is spelt normally. *Ils* and *els* for a feminine plural existed in the middle ages.

Envoi. The envoi needs careful translation. The "que" of the third line = "sans que" and the whole means, "Do not ask this week or this year where they are, *without* letting this refrain haunt you." "Que" might possibly mean "de peur que," did not the whole sense of the poem forbid such an interpretation.

NOTES.

An Excerpt from the Grant Testament.

Stanza 75, line 4. A charming example of those "flashes" which reveal Villon.

Stanza 76, line 2. Note the spelling of *Grant* in the feminine without an *e*. Adjectives of the third declension whose feminine was not distinguishable in Latin took no "e" in early French. A survival of this is found in grand' rue, grand' messe, etc.

Line 5. *Grant erre*, "quickly," and the whole line reads: "Let it (my body) be delivered to it (luy=la terre) quickly," the "erre" here is from the popular late Latin "*iterare*" = "*iter facere*." It survives in the nautical idiom "reprendre son erre "="to get under weigh again."

Line 7. "*Erre*" here comes, on the contrary, from *errare*, to make a mistake, to err.

Stanza 77, line 4. *Maillon*. Swaddling clothes.

Line 5. *Boullon*, scrape. The two lines are obscure but seem to read: "He has got me out of many a scrape which gave him no joy" (*esioye* from *esjouir* = *rejouir*).

Line 7 and 8. These are obscure but apparently="And beseech him on my knees not to forsake all joy on that account."

Stanza 78, line 2. "*Le Romman du Pet au Deable.*" The Pet au Deable was a great stone at the door of a private house in the university. The students took it away and all Paris fought over the matter. The "Roman" was a set of verses, now lost, which Villon wrote on the quarrel.

Line 3. *Guy Tabarie* who *grossa* (wrote out), these verses was a friend of Villon's: soon hanged.

Line 5. *Soubz*. The "b" is pedantic, the *ou* indicates of itself the loss of the *b*. The "z" (and the "s" in the modern *sous*) are due to the derivation not from *sub* but *subtus*.

The Ballad of Our Lady.

Stanza 2, line 3. *Egypcienne*. St. Mary of Egypt.

Line 4. *Theophilus*. This was that clerk who sold his soul to the Devil and whom Our Lady redeemed. You may find the whole story

NOTES.

sculptured on the Tympanum of the exquisite northern door of Notre Dame in Paris.

Line 8. *Vierge Portant*=" Virgin that bore a son."

Stanza 3, line 4. *Luz*="luthus." " S " becomes " z."

The Envoi. Note the Acrostic " Villon " in the first letters of the first six lines. It is a trick he played more than once.

THE DEAD LORDS.

Stanza 1, line 1. *Calixte.* These names are of less interest. *Calixte* was Pope Calixtus III., Alphonso Borgia, who died in 1458—in Villon's twenty-sixth year. *Alphonse* is Alphonso V. of Arragon, who died in that same year. The *Duc de Bourbon* is Charles the First of Bourbon, who died at the end of the year 1456, "gracieux" because his son protected Villon. *Artus* (Arthur) of Brittany is that same Richemont who recaptured Paris from Willoughby. Charles VII. is Charles VII. The *Roy Scotiste* is James II., who died in 1460: the *Amethyst* half of his face was a birthmark. The *King of Cyprus* is probably John III., who died in that same fatal year, 1458. Pedants will have it that the *King of Spain* is John II. of Castille, who died in 1454—but it is a better joke if it means nobody at all. *Lancelot* is Vladislas of Bohemia, who died in 1457. *Cloquin* is Bertrand de Guesclin who led the reconquest. *The Count Daulphin* of Auvergne is doubtful; *Alençon* is presumably the Alençon of Joan of Arc's campaign, who still survived, and is called "feu " half in ridicule, because in 1458 he had lost his title and lands for treason.

Stanza 2, line 3. *Amatiste*=amethyst.

Stanza 3, line 7. *Tayon*=Ancestor. "*Etallum.*" Latin " *Stallio.*"

THE DIRGE.

Line 1. *Cil*=celui-ci. The Latin " *ecce illum.*"

Line 3. *Escuelle*=bowl. "With neither bowl nor platter."

Line 4. Note again the constant redundant negative of the populace in this scholar: "Had never, no—not a sprig of parsley."

Line 5. *Rez*=ras, cropped.

NOTES.

MAROT.

OF COURTING LONG AGO.

Line 5. *On se prenoit*, one attacked—"it was but the heart one sought."

Line 11. *Fainɕtz*=sham; "*changes*" is simply like the English "changes": the form survives in the idiom: "donner le change."

Line 13. *Refonde*=recast.

NOËL.

Verse 1, line 3. *L'Autre hyer*= alterum heri, "t'other day."

Line 10. *Noé.* The tendency to drop final letters, especially the *l*, is very marked in popular patois, and this is, of course, a song based on popular language. Most French peasants north of the Loire would still say "Noé" for "Noël." *Noël* is, of course, *Natalem* (diem).

Verse 2, Line 2. *Cas de si hault faiɕt*=so great a matter.

TWO EPIGRAMS.

Epigram 1, line 2. *Vostre.* Marguerite of Navarre. As I have remarked, in the text, she had sent him a Dixaine (some say he wrote it himself). This one is written in answer.—*Ay.* Note, till the verb grew over simple in the classical French of the seventeenth century there was no more need for the pronoun than in Latin. Thus Montaigne will omit the pronoun, but Malherbe never.

Line 5. *Cuydans*=thinking (*Cogitare*=*Cogtare*=*Coyde*=*cuider*, the *oi* became *ui* by a common transition; *cf.* noɕtem, oɕtem, noit, nuit, huit.) The word is now archaic.

Line 9. *Encor.* Without the final e. This is not archaic but poetic licence. *Encore*="hanc horam," and a post tonic "am" in Latin always means a final mute e in French.

Epigram 2, line 1. *Maint* (now archaic) is a word of Teutonic origin, our *many*.

Line 6. *Coulpe*=Culpam, of course; a fault.

232

NOTES.

Line 9. *Emport.* Note the old subjunctive without the final e. *Vide supra*, on "*Chant.*" The modern usage is incorrect. For the first conjugation making its subjunctive in *em*, should lose the final syllable in French: a post tonic *em* always disappears. The modern habit of putting a final e to all subjunctives is due to a false analogy with verbs from the third conjugation. These made their subjunctive in *am*, a termination which properly becomes the mute e of French.

To His Lady in Sickness.

Line 4. *Sejour*=(here) "staying at home."

Line 14, 15. *Friande de la bouche*, glutton.

Line 17. *Danger.* The first meaning of "Danger" is simply "to be in lordship" (Dominicarium). The modern is the English "Danger." This is between the two; "held to your hurt."

Line 26. *Doint.* This subjunctive should properly be *don* (*donem*, post tonic *em* is lost). The "oint" is from a false analogy with the fourth conjugation, as though the Latin had been *doniam.*

The Vineyard Song.

Verse 1, line 2. *Clamours.* See how southern this is, with its Lanquedoc forms, "clamours" for "clam*eurs*."

Line 5. So are these diminutions all made up at random, as southern as can be, and note the tang of the verse, fit for a snapping of the fingers to mark the rapid time.

Verse 3, line 2. *Bénistre.* The older form of *bénir* from *Benedicere;* the *c* between vowels at the end of the tonic syllable becomes *s*: the *t* is added for euphony, to help one to pronounce the *s.*

Line 3. *Silenus* for *Silène.* Because the name was new, the Latin form is kept. The genius of the French, unlike that of modern English, is to absorb a foreign name (as we did once). Thus once we said "Anthony" "Tully": but Montaigne wrote "Cicero"—his descendants say "Ciceron."

NOTES.

Line 4. *Aussi droiɕt qu'une ligne*="right out of the flask." The flask held above one and the wine poured straight into the mouth. The happy south still know the way.

Line 5. *Bigne:* a lump, a knock, a bruise.

Line 6. *Guigne*=cherry.

RONSARD.

DIALOGUE WITH THE NINE SISTERS.

Stanza 1, line 3. *Chef grison*=gray head. When he says "trente ans," that is all rubbish, he was getting on for forty-three: it was written in 1567.

Stanza 2, line 1. *Nocher*=pilot; rare but hardly archaic.

Stanza 3, line 3. *Cependant*=meanwhile. The word is now seldom used in prose, save in the sense of "notwithstanding," "nevertheless."

Stanza 5, line 1. *Loyer*=Condition of tenure.

Line 2. *Ores*=Now that. Should be "*ore*" (horam). The parasitic "s" probably crept in by false analogy with the adverbs in "s."

Stanza 6, line 1. *Lame* = tombstone. The word is no longer used.

Line 4. See how, even in his lighter or prosaic manner, he cannot avoid great lines.

Stanza 8, line 1. *Vela*=Voilà. Then follows that fine ending which I have put on the title-page of this book.

"MIGNONNE ALLONS VOIR SI LA ROSE."

Line 1. *Mignonne* is, of course, his Cassandre: her personality was always known through his own verse. She was fifteen when he met her and her brown eyes: it was in 1546 at Blois, her birthplace, whither he had gone to visit the Court, during his scholar's life in Paris. He met her thus young when he himself was but in his twenty-third year, and all that early, violent, not over-tilled beginning of his poetry was illumined by her face. But as to who she was, by name I mean, remained long a

234

matter of doubt. Binet would have it that her true name was Cassandre, and that its singularity inspired Ronsard. Brantôme called it " a false name to cover a true." Ronsard himself has written, " false or true, time conquering all things cannot efface it from the marble." There need have been no doubt. D'Aubigné's testimony is sufficient. She was a Mlle. de Pie, and such was the vagary of Ronsard's life, that it was her niece, Diane Salviati de Taley whom in later life he espoused and nearly wed.

Line 3. Note *Pourpre*, and in line 5 *Pourprée* so in line 9 *Beautez*, and in the last line *Beauté:* so little did he fear repetition and so heartily could his power carry it.

Line 4. *A point:* the language was still in flux. The phrase would require a negative *n'* in modern French.

Line 10, 11. *Marastre . . . puisqu'une . .* There is here an elliptical construction never found in later French. Harsh stepmother nature (whom I call harsh) since . . . " etc.

SONNETS FOR HÉLÈNE.

Sonnet xlii., line 1. *Ocieuse=* " otiosa," langorous.

Line 5. *Ennuy*, in the sixteenth century meant something fuller than, and somewhat different from the word " ennui " to-day. It was a weariness which had in it some permanent chagrin.

Line 8. *Pipe*, " cajoles ": a word which (now that it is unusual) mars the effect of its meaning by its insignificant sound.

Lines 8 and 9. Note *ioye, vraye*, a feminine " e " following another vowel is, since Malherbe, forbidden in the interior of a verse, unless elided.

Line 11. *Ton mort*, " your ghost."

Sonnet xliii., line 6. *Desia=*déjà.

Line 7. *De mon nom.* I have printed the line thus because Ronsard himself wished it so, and so corrected it with his own hand. But the original form is far finer *"Au bruit de Ronsard."*

NOTES.

DU BELLAY.

THE SONNET "HEUREUX QUI COMME ULYSSE."

Line 3. *Usage.* A most powerful word in this slightly archaic sense: the experience of long travel: familiar knowledge of things seen.

Line 12. *Loire.* This word has puzzled more than one editor. There are two rivers: the great river Loire, which is feminine, and the little Loir, which is masculine. Here Du Bellay spells the name of the great river, but puts it in the masculine gender. It has been imagined that he was talking of the smaller river. But he was not. The Loire alone has any connection with Liré or with his life, and as for the gender, strained as the interpretation may seem, I believe that Du Bellay deliberately used it in the parallel with the Tiber and the idea of the "Fleuve Paternel," to which he alludes so often elsewhere.

Line 13. *Lyré.* The modern Liré, his birthplace, on the left bank of the Loire, just opposite Ancenis. As you go along the Poitiers road to the bridge it stands up on your right, just before the river.

THE DOG.

Line 1. *Motte*=a turf.

Line 40. *Damoiselet.* Still used more or less in its old sense of a young man *armed:* not mereley a young page or a cadet of the gentry,="like a little sentry."

Line 43. *Anvie*=(of course) "envie."

THE CAT.

Line 22. *Rouët*=spinning-wheel.

Line 26. *Panne*=the Italian *Panno*—cloth.

Line 27. *Troigne*=the mouth and face of an animal, the muzzle.

Line 32. *Chere*=(originally) "head" and one of the few old French words derived from Greek, but the first signification has long been lost. Here the phrase is equivalent to "faire bonne chere" which has for centuries been used proverbially for what we call "a good time." *V. supra* in "The Farewell" of Charles of Orleans.

NOTES.

MALHERBE.

Extracts from the "Ode to Louis XIII."

Stanza 3, line 1. *Centième.* He dates the Huguenot trouble from a century. It may be said to have originated in the placards threatening the defilement of the Sacrament, placards which appeared in the streets of Paris in 1525.

Stanza 2, line 3. *Le nom de Juste.* Louis XIII. had no particular affectation of that title: it is rather a reminiscence of his distant collatoral and namesake who closed the fifteenth century.

Last stanza, line 1. *Toutes les autres morts.* He has just been speaking of death in battle against the factions.

Sonnet on His Son's Death.

Line 1. *Mon fils.* The only survivor of his many children, a young man, just called to the bar at Aix and passionately loved by his father, he bore the curious name of Marc-Anthony. A M. de Piles killed him in a duel, having for second his brother-in-law. The whole was an honourable bit of business, and the death such as men of honour must be prepared to risk: but Malherbe would see no reason and defamed the adversary.

Line 9. *La Raison.* The idea runs all through Malherbe's work. It is his distinguishing note, and is the spirit which differentiates him so powerfully from the sixteenth century, that this stoical balance or regulator which he calls "La Raison," and which governed France for two hundred years, is his rule and text for verse and prose as well as for practical life. Even the grandeur to which it gave rise seemed to him accidental. He demanded "la raison" only, and felt the necessity of it in art as acutely as though its absence were something immoral.

Extracts from the "Consolation of du Perrier."

Stanza 1, line 1. *Duperrier.* A critic of sorts and a gentleman, living in Provence and perhaps of Provencal ancestry. The verses were written while Malherbe's fame was still local, two years before the king's visit had lifted him to Paris.

Stanza 2, line 2. *Ta fille.* The child Marguerite. Her name does not appear in the poem nor in any letter; we have it from Racan.

Stanza 10, line 3. *Et la garde, etc.* These two lines are quoted, sometimes, not often, by admirers who would prove that Malherbe was not incapable of colour or of warmth.